Office Skills

Combined text

NVQ Accounting Units 21, 22 & 23

Michael Fardon

Roger Petheram

osborne
BOOKS

Published by Osborne Books Limited
Unit 1B Everoak Estate
Bromyard Road
Worcester WR2 5HP
Tel 01905 748071
Email books@osbornebooks.co.uk
Website www.osbornebooks.co.uk

Design by Richard Holt
Cover image from Getty Images

Printed by the Bath Press, Bath

British Library Cataloguing in Publication Data
A catalogue record for this book is available from the British Library

ISBN 1 872962 36 X

Contents

Acknowledgements

The authors wish to thank the following for their help with the production of the text and illustrations in this book: Rob Fardon, Mike Gilbert, Claire McCarthy, and Liz Smith. Thanks also go to Steve Tubb for advice on the technical aspects of Health & Safety and to Wendy Yates for sharing her 'working with computers' expertise.

The publisher would also like to thank Ann Fontbin and Debbie Board, both experienced AAT lecturers, who tested the Sage computer accounting exercises and also advised on the assessment requirements of the NVQ Units covered.

The publisher is indebted to the Association of Accounting Technicians for its generous help and advice to our authors and editors during the preparation of this text, and for permission to reproduce extracts from the Standards of Competence for Accounting and also a page from its website. Thanks also go to Accounting Technician (AAT's magazine) and the Health and Safety Executive for permission to reproduce web pages.

Authors

Michael Fardon has extensive teaching experience of a wide range of banking, business and accountancy courses at Worcester College of Technology. He now specialises in writing business and financial texts and is General Editor at Osborne Books. He is also an educational consultant and has worked extensively in the areas of vocational business curriculum development.

Roger Petheram has lectured at Worcester College of Technology on a wide range of accounting, business and management courses for a number of years. He previously worked as a senior accountant for the Health Service. He is currently senior editor for accounting texts at Osborne Books, with particular responsibility for the AAT Series.

Introduction

Office Skills has been written to cover the requirements of the revised 2003 NVQ Accounting standards. It is a study resource for students achieving competence in:

Unit 21	Working with Computers
Unit 22	Contribute to the maintenance of a healthy, safe and productive working environment
Unit 23	Achieving personal effectiveness

a 'combined' text

Office Skills is a 'combined' text in two parts. The **first part** consists of a series of chapters providing the knowledge and understanding needed for the three Units. These chapters contain:

- a clear text with numerous Case Studies
- a chapter summary and key terms
- student activities – with answers provided

This first section of the text – with questions and answers – is therefore useful for classroom use and also for distance learning students.

assessment material

The **second part** of the text guides students in the collection of Portfolio evidence, ideally from the workplace.

It is appreciated that some students are in employment, some have work experience placements, while others experience more difficulty in gathering workplace evidence. This last category of student may turn instead to voluntary organisations and even to the teaching Centre itself (although using the Centre is not generally recommended).

The solution adopted by the authors is to provide alternative methods of evidence collection for students:

- where the student is in the workplace – **witness statements** where the workplace manager confirms the student's competence in each performance criterion and item of the range (note: these may be photocopied)
- where the student is unable to obtain workplace evidence – **simulations** based on Case Study material and questioning

integration of Unit 21

It is recommended that the evidence for Unit 21 'Working with Computers' is obtained in part through practical computer exercises carried out to generate evidence for other Units:

- coverage of the range at Level 2 for Units 1, 2, 3 and 4 (computer accounting, word processing and spreadsheets)
- coverage of the range at Level 3 for direct entry students taking Unit 7 (spreadsheet and word processed report)

The Assessment Guidance for Unit 21 at the back of this book provides simulations for Level 2 students and also for students entering the scheme at Level 3.

The Level 2 simulation is based on the widely-used Sage computer accounting software. Osborne Books has prepared a set-up file which will enable Centres to load all the details of the simulated company on the computer system. If you would like a copy of this file, please telephone Osborne Books Customer Services on 01905 748071.

feedback

If you have any feedback on the content of this book, or suggestions about the delivery of the Units, please feel free to contact our editorial team on 01905 748071.

Michael Fardon

Roger Petheram

Summer 2003

Coverage of NVQ Standards

UNIT 21: WORKING WITH COMPUTERS

Element 21.1: Use computer systems and software

Performance Criteria   *chapter*

A   Perform initial visual safety checks and power up the computer system   1

B   Use passwords to gain access to the computer system where limitations on access to   1
    data is required

C   Access, save and print data files and exit from relevant software   1

D   Use appropriate file names and save work   1

E   Back up work carried out on a computer system to suitable storage media at regular   1
    intervals

F   Close down the computer without damaging the computer system   1

G   Seek immediate assistance when difficulties occur   1

Element 21.2: Maintain the security of data

Performance Criteria

A   Ensure passwords are kept secret and changed at appropriate times   2

B   Ensure computer hardware and program disks are kept securely located   2

C   Identify potential risks to data from different sources and take steps to resolve or   2
    minimise them

D   Maintain security and confidentiality of data at all times   2

E   Understand and implement relevant legal regulations   2

UNIT 22: CONTRIBUTE TO THE MAINTENANCE OF A HEALTHY, SAFE AND PRODUCTIVE WORKING ENVIRONMENT

Element 22.1: Monitor and maintain a safe, healthy and secure working environment

Performance Criteria

		chapter
A	Make sure you read, comply with and have up-to-date information on the health, safety and security requirements and procedures for your workplace	3,4
B	Make sure that the procedures are being followed and report any that are not to the relevant person	4
C	Identify and correct any hazards that you can deal with safely, competently and within the limits of your authority	4
D	Promptly and accurately report any hazards that you are not allowed to deal with to the relevant person and warn other people who may be affected	4
E	Follow your organisation's emergency procedures promptly, calmly and efficiently	5
F	Identify and recommend opportunities for improving health, safety and security to the responsible person	4
G	Complete any health and safety records legibly and accurately	5

Element 22.2: Monitor and maintain an effective and efficient working environment

Performance Criteria

A	Organise the work area you are responsible for, so that you and others can work efficiently	6
B	Organise the work area you are responsible for, so that it meets your organisation's requirements and presents a positive image of yourself and your team	6
C	Identify conditions around you that interfere with effective working	6
D	Put right any conditions that you can deal with safely, competently, within the limits of your authority and with the agreement of other relevant people	6
E	Promptly and accurately report any other conditions to the relevant person	6
F	Use and maintain equipment in accordance with manufacturer's instructions and your organisation's procedures	6

UNIT 23: ACHIEVING PERSONAL EFFECTIVENESS

Element 23.1: Plan and organise your own work

Performance Criteria

chapter

A	Identify and prioritise tasks according to organisational procedures and regulatory requirements	7
B	Recognise changes in priorities and adapt resources allocations and work plans accordingly	7
C	Use appropriate planning aids to plan and monitor work progress	7
D	Identify, negotiate and co-ordinate relevant assistance to meet specific demands and deadlines	7
E	Report anticipated difficulties in meeting deadlines to the appropriate person	7
F	Check that work methods and activities conform to legal and regulatory requirements and organisational procedures	7

Element 23.2: Maintain good working relationships

Performance Criteria

A	Communicate with other people clearly and effectively, using your organisation's procedures	8
B	Discuss and agree realistic objectives, resources, working methods and schedules and in a way that promotes good working relationships	8
C	Meet commitments to colleagues within agreed timescales	8
D	Offer assistance and support where colleagues cannot meet deadlines, within your own work constraints and other commitments	8
E	Find workable solutions for any conflicts and dissatisfaction which reduce personal and team effectiveness	8
F	Follow organisational procedures if there are difficulties in working relationships that are beyond your authority or ability to resolve, and promptly refer them to the appropriate person	8
G	Treat others courteously and work in a way that shows respect for other people	8
H	Ensure data protection requirements are followed strictly and also maintain confidentiality of information relating to colleagues	8

Element 23.3: Improve your own performance

Performance Criteria

chapter

A   Identify your own development needs by taking into consideration your current work activities and also your own career goals   9

B   Define your own development objectives and, where necessary, agree them with the appropriate person   9

C   Research appropriate ways of acquiring new skills and knowledge   9

D   Ensure that development opportunities are realistic and achievable in terms of resources and support from relevant persons   9

E   Review and evaluate your performance and progress and also to agreed timescales   9

F   Monitor your own understanding of developments relating to your job role   9

G   Maintain and develop your own specialist knowledge relevant to your own working environment   9

H   Undertake learning that will help you improve your performance   9

Unit 21

Working with computers

what this unit is about

This unit is about your ability to use a computer system safely and effectively. For the first element, you will need to demonstrate that you are fully aware of your responsibilities when using a computer system and the software packages you will need. For the second element you will be required to show an understanding of the need to keep data confidential and secure.

The Unit is covered by two chapters:

Element 21.1   Chapter 1   **Computer systems and software**

Element 21.2   Chapter 2   **Data security**

1 Computer systems and software

this chapter covers . . .

This chapter introduces the basics of computer systems – the hardware and the software used. It deals with the skills needed for the everyday use of computers and computer programs. These include:

- the procedures for starting up and shutting down a computer system
- the use of passwords
- how to use the software: opening, transferring and printing files
- saving data and maintaining systems for backing up
- knowing what to do when something goes wrong

NVQ PERFORMANCE CRITERIA COVERED

unit 21: WORKING WITH COMPUTERS
element 21.1
Use computer systems and software

A   perform initial visual safety checks and power up the computer system

B   use passwords to gain access to the computer system where limitations on access to data is required

C   access, save and print data files and exit from relevant software

D   use appropriate file names and save work

E   back up work carried out on a computer system to suitable storage media at regular intervals

F   close down the computer without damaging the computer system

G   seek immediate assistance when difficulties occur

COMPUTER SYSTEMS

This first section of the chapter may seem to be stating what is generally well known, so apologies to readers who are computer 'savvy' experts.

A computer system comprises both 'hardware' and 'software'.

Computer **hardware** is the equipment which makes up the computer system. It comprises:

- the main processing unit (often housed in a 'tower') which runs the programs and stores the data
- a screen (monitor)
- keyboard
- mouse
- peripherals (add ons) such as printers, scanners and back-up devices

Computer **software** comprises the programs – such as wordprocessing, spreadsheets, databases, accounting programs – which run through the operating system on the hardware.

There are two main ways of setting up the hardware – a standalone system and a network.

standalone system

A typical standalone system uses a single main processing unit with a screen, mouse, a back-up device for data storage and a printer and scanner. This computer is likely be linked to the internet by phone line. This type of system is useful for a small business when only one person needs to operate the computer at any one time.

network and intranet

A **network** comprises a number of computer workstations linked to a server (which holds all the data) and other equipment such as printers and scanners. This type of system is likely to be used by a larger business or organisation (such as a college IT centre) where a number of operators need to access the system and its data at the same time. A network will often give employees direct access to the internet through an **internet** service provider.

When a network is set up, it is also possible to establish an **intranet**. This is an internal website which operates through the network and enables employees to share data, documents and internal web pages. An intranet cannot be accessed by outsiders.

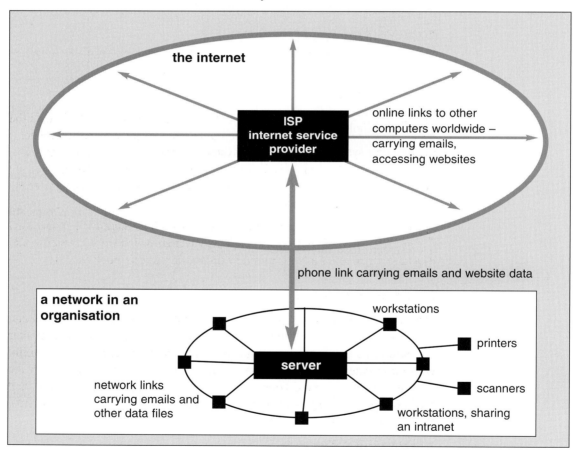

printers

All computer systems need a printer to produce 'hard copy' such as letters, financial documents and management reports. The old-fashioned form of printer is the dot matrix printer which prints text as a series of dots using a printer head with pins. This is useful if you need multiple copies of documents such as invoices: the pins strike the paper with enough force to print the characters through a number of sheets of paper. If better quality printing is required an inkjet or laser printer can be used.

data storage and backup

It is very important that the data held by the computer is backed up regularly and stored away from the premises or transmitted to another location. Data can be backed up onto a variety of storage media, eg floppy disk, zip disk, tape, CD and DVD. All systems should therefore have some form of data storage facility or be able to transmit data to another location.

COMPUTER SOFTWARE

windows operating systems

The program – the **software** – that makes a computer work is known as the operating system. Most business computers are PCs (personal computers) running the Windows operating system which is a Microsoft product. Another Microsoft product is the Office suite of programs which includes the Word word processing program, the Excel spreadsheet, the Access database and the Powerpoint presentation program.

Standard 'off-the-shelf' accounting programs such as Sage Line 50 are also designed for use in Windows, and it is this system which we will refer to and illustrate when referring to computer accounting in this book.

types of software

We will now outline the different types of software used in businesses and other organisations and then explain how they 'fit in' with computer accounting packages such as Sage. It may be that you are already familiar with these types of program. Even so it is a good idea to read through the next few pages to remind yourself of the exact function of the packages and see how they can be integrated with computer accounting software. The main types of program are:

- word processing
- databases
- spreadsheets
- email managers
- accounting packages
- web browsers

WORD PROCESSING

Word processing programs – including Microsoft Word – enable you to

- enter text
- format text, eg set it out in columns, add bullet points
- change and edit text
- set up tables

Word processed text can be saved and printed out in the form of letters, memos, reports, and notices. These will normally be in a set format known as the organisation's **house style**. The word-processing files will act as templates which can be used throughout the organisation when a document is required. Word processed text can be sent electronically either on disk, or as an attachment file on an email. Some text in Osborne Books' publications is first input in Word and sent in on disk or by email by its authors.

Word processing programs can be linked up with other programs. For example, the names and addresses from a computer accounting package can be imported to 'mailmerge' into a set of letters sent out to customers. Also, a spreadsheet can be integrated into a word processing document in an integrated suite of programs such as Microsoft Office.

The screen below shows how the original version of some of the text on this page was set up in Word and then imported into a page layout program used in publishing.

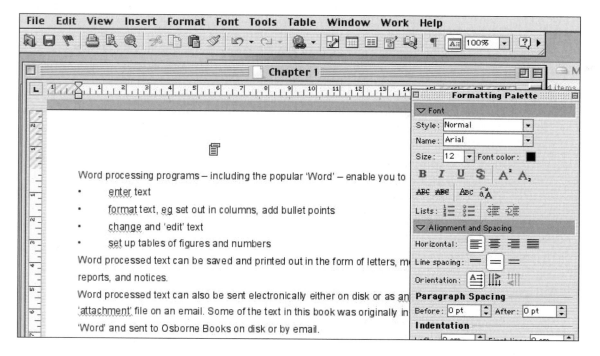

DATABASES

A computer database enables you to input and store information in an organised way so that it can be readily accessed, sorted and exported. A database is essentially an electronic filing system which takes all the hard work out of sorting and retrieving information.

Imagine, for example, your business does not have a computer database. It keeps the names and addresses of 250 customers on cards sorted alphabetically by surname and kept in a plastic box in the office. Suppose

- you drop the box on the floor and all the cards get out of order, or
- you are asked to identify all the customers who are based in Nottingham
  These two situations will take a long time to sort out if the records are kept on cards. If this information were stored on a computer database . . .
- the records could automatically be sorted alphabetically by surname
- you could ask the computer to search the field which contains the town or city name which is 'Nottingham'

Note that two terms are used here:

- a record is a set of information which corresponds to each card in a card index – here it is a customer record which is likely to contain the name of the customer, address, telephone number, and email
- a field is a part of the record (normally a box to fill in on the computer screen) which contains a specific piece of information, for example, customer surname, town, telephone number, email

A customer record is shown in the screen below. Note how the information is stored in different fields. In particular, note how the address is a series of fields. The 'Town/City' field is one of these.

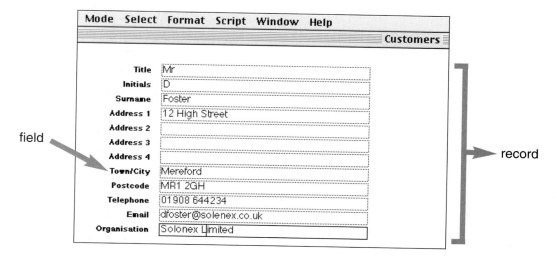

using data

Databases are very useful if you wish to record and make use of significant data relating to your business or organisation. For example, assume that the 'Customers' record shown on the previous page is part of a list of the people and organisations to whom a business sells its products. It could be expanded with further fields to record information such as:

- date last contacted
- status – eg target customers (those who have not ordered)
- details of products sold

The 'Customers' file could then be accessed and searched to produce lists, for example, of customers not contacted within the last six months, target customers and customers who have bought a particular product.

The possibilities offered by a database apply to many areas. The index of this book, for example, was created by a database which alphabetically sorts fields containing text.

SPREADSHEETS

calculations

A spreadsheet is a grid of boxes – 'cells' – set up on the computer, organised in rows and columns into which you can enter text and numbers. The computer program will work out the calculations automatically once you have entered an appropriate formula in the cell where the result of the calculations is required. The great advantage of a spreadsheet is that it enables you to manipulate and analyse large quantities of numerical data.

Another advantage of a spreadsheet is that if you change any of the figures, the computer will automatically recalculate the total, saving you much time and effort.

Spreadsheets are used for a variety of functions in organisations:

- working out the cost of products
- working out budget forecasts
- working out sales figures for different products or areas

A commonly used spreadsheet program is Microsoft Excel. The example on the next page shows regional sales figures input into Excel. Note that the rows are numbered and the columns have letter references. The total sales figure appears in the cell (box) which therefore has the reference of B11.

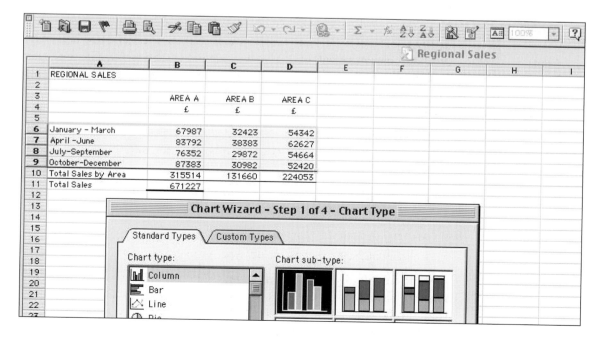

	A	B	C	D	E	F	G
1	REGIONAL SALES						
2							
3		AREA A	AREA B	AREA C			
4		£	£	£			
5							
6	January – March	67987	32423	54342			
7	April –June	83792	38383	62627			
8	July-September	76352	29872	54664			
9	October-December	87383	30982	52420			
10	Total Sales by Area	315514	131660	224053			
11	Total Sales	671227					
12							
13							

producing graphs and charts

Another function of the spreadsheet is its ability to produce graphs and charts from the figures in the spreadsheet grid. All that you need to do is to select the appropriate figures and the computer does the rest through its charting function. Look at the screens below and on the next page which use the sales figures illustrated in the screen above. Note how the cells have been selected and highlighted.

	A	B	C	D	E	F	G	H	I
1	REGIONAL SALES								
2									
3		AREA A	AREA B	AREA C					
4		£	£	£					
5									
6	January – March	67987	32423	54342					
7	April –June	83792	38383	62627					
8	July-September	76352	29872	54664					
9	October-December	87383	30982	52420					
10	Total Sales by Area	315514	131660	224053					
11	Total Sales	671227							
12									
13									

Chart Wizard – Step 1 of 4 – Chart Type

Standard Types / Custom Types

Chart type:
- Column
- Bar
- Line
- Pie

Chart sub-type:

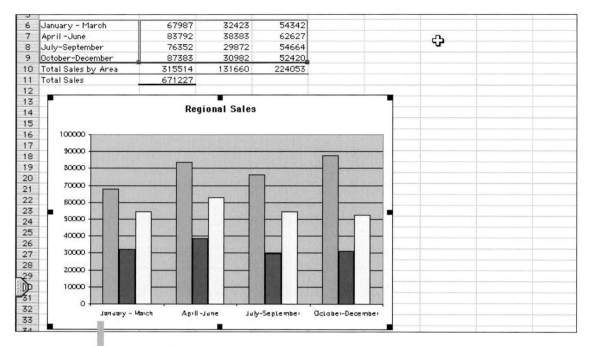

using the chart

The chart can then be copied and pasted into a word processing document, in this case a Sales Report memorandum.

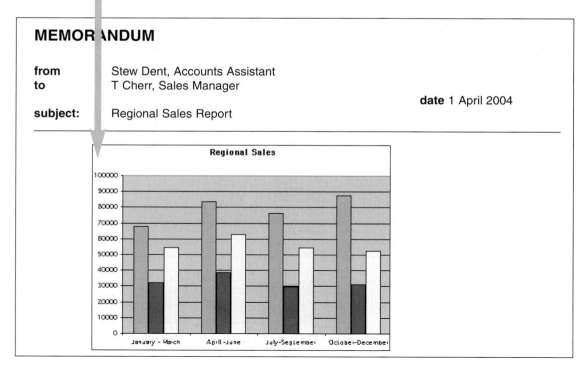

EMAIL MANAGEMENT

Most businesses and other organisations are now connected to the internet and can send and receive external emails. Some businesses and other organisations also communicate through an intranet and can send emails internally. Another important computer program is therefore the email management system. Common examples are Outlook and Groupwise. The screen below shows the outbox, which shows you messages sent and about to be sent. In this case a message is going to Osborne Books, the publishers of this book.

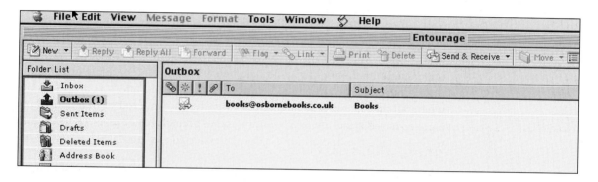

uses of email and attachments

Email is a very useful and inexpensive means of sending messages electronically not only within a business but also externally to customers and suppliers. Transmission is instantaneous. This can be an advantage, but can also be a disadvantage – it often demands a rapid reply.

Email enables you to send many types of file as 'attachments', such as word processing, database and spreadsheet files, from one computer to another.

Documents – orders and invoices for example – can be generated on the computer and sent by email attachment to suppliers and customers.

electronic documents and EDI

Data and documents – eg financial documents such as orders and invoices – can also be sent electronically through Electronic Data Interchange (EDI) programs. This form of transfer – which has been in use for a number of years – employs software which is more specialised (ie expensive!) than the normal email management programs already mentioned. The principle, however, is the same – electronic documentation. The process is reliable, fast and efficient and often used by supermarket chains in ordering and paying for goods.

INTRODUCTION TO COMPUTER ACCOUNTING PACKAGES

a growth area

Although some organisations, particularly small businesses, still use paper-based accounting systems, an increasing number are now operating computerised accounting systems. Businesses can buy 'off-the shelf' accounting programs from suppliers such as Sage, and customise them to their particular needs

links with traditional book-keeping

You will know that your study of book-keeping and accounts concentrates largely on paper-based systems. The reason for this is that when you use a paper-based system you have to do all the work manually, so you can understand the theory that underlies the system: you prepare the documents, make entries in the accounts, balance the cash book, and so on. You know where all the figures are entered, and why they are entered. If you know how a paper-based system works, you will be in a much better position to be able to understand the operation of a computer-based system.

comparison with other types of computer program

Computer accounting packages – such as the Sage Line 50 series of products – make use of many of the functions of the other types of computer program already described in this chapter. Most computer accounting packages contain:

- word processing functions – eg the facility to write memos and notes
- a series of databases – eg details of customers, stock items held
- calculation facilities – eg invoices where the operator inputs figures and the program automatically generates VAT amounts and totals
- charting and graphing facilities – eg charting of activity on a customer account

facilities

A typical computer accounting program will offer a number of facilities:

- on-screen input and printout of sales invoices and credit notes
- automatic updating of customer accounts with sales transactions
- recording of suppliers' invoices
- automatic updating of supplier accounts with details of purchases
- recording of money paid into the bank
- recording of payments to suppliers and for expenses

management reports

A computer accounting program can provide instant reports for management, for example:

- an aged debtors' summary – showing who owes you what and for what periods of time
- activity reports on customer and supplier accounts
- activity reports on expenses accounts

advantages of a computer accounting program

Computer accounting programs, like the other computer programs outlined in this chapter, are popular because they offer a number of distinct advantages over paper-based systems:

- they tend to be more accurate because they rely on single-entry input (one amount per transaction) rather than double-entry book-keeping
- they can provide the accounting function of the organisation with a clear and up-to-date picture of what is happening
- they can print VAT Returns and other useful reports for management
- they save time, and therefore money

The diagram below shows a menu bar setting out the structure of a Sage computer accounting program.

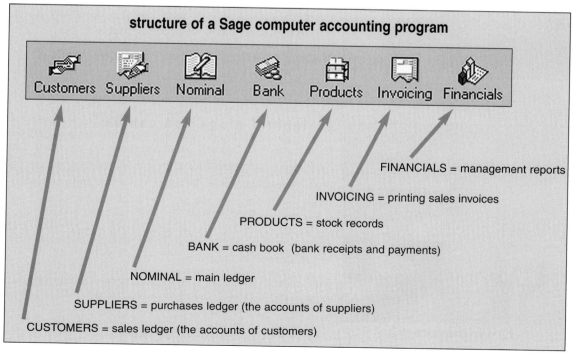

structure of a Sage computer accounting program

Customers   Suppliers   Nominal   Bank   Products   Invoicing   Financials

FINANCIALS = management reports

INVOICING = printing sales invoices

PRODUCTS = stock records

BANK = cash book (bank receipts and payments)

NOMINAL = main ledger

SUPPLIERS = purchases ledger (the accounts of suppliers)

CUSTOMERS = sales ledger (the accounts of customers)

STARTING UP A COMPUTER SYSTEM

There are a number of visual safety checks that you must perform when starting up a computer system.

hardware components

Are all the hardware components there? Check to see if the main processing unit and peripherals such as screens, printers, back-up drives and scanners are in place and have not been moved by a cleaner or removed for maintenance, or worse still, by a thief!

If there is a problem, you should refer it to someone in a position of responsibility who will be able to deal with it. Clearly if equipment is missing, it will need to be dealt with urgently.

have you checked the power supply?

power plugs

Is everything plugged in correctly? Check the following:

- are the mains plugs in place and is the electrical supply up and running?

- check any power supply surge protectors are correctly in place (these protect against surges in current which might damage sensitive electronic devices such as computers)

- are the mains plugs plugged in properly?

If there is any problem here you should either fix it yourself if you are able, or refer it to someone in a position of responsibility who will be able to deal with it.

peripheral plugs and cables

In a standalone system (one computer on its own) the main processing unit should be connected to a variety of devices such as mouse, keyboard, monitor and peripheral units such as printer, scanner and back-up device such as a zip drive.

A quick visual check will tell you whether these devices are all securely plugged in.

You should also check that the internet connection is plugged in.

are you connected?

If you are working on a network system you will need to check your work station connections. Peripheral devices such as printers may be situated elsewhere in the office and will not be connected directly to your machine. In this case you will be able to check on screen once the computer is up and running.

Lastly, and very importantly, check that cables are not positioned dangerously, where people could trip over them and possibly injure themselves. This is part of your personal responsibility under the Health and Safety regulations (see Chapter 3). You may be able to deal with dangerous cabling yourself, or, if you are not able to put it right, you should refer the problem to someone in a position of responsibility who will be able to deal with it.

powering up

When all these checks have been carried out, you should switch on the computer(s) in the usual way and hopefully experience a trouble-free session operating the computer system.

USING PASSWORDS

Before getting going on the computer you are likely to have to use **passwords** to enable you to gain access to:

- the computer itself, for example if you are using a workstation on a network – this is a **system password**
- particular computer programs, some of which may enable you to access sensitive or confidential information – eg the accounting software – this is a **software password**

We will deal with the security aspect of passwords in the next chapter. We will concentrate here on the practical aspects of passwords as part of the starting up procedure.

system passwords – logging on

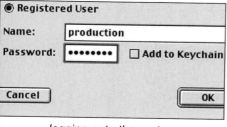

logging onto the system

If you are working on a network you have to 'log on' as a user before you can use a computer workstation. You may have to give a user name and also a unique password. The user name will normally show on the screen as you input it, but the password will show as a series of dots or asterisks. The example on the left shows someone logging onto a computer in the production department. Logging on is a simple process, and you may well be familiar with it because it is normally used when you log onto the internet.

software passwords – accessing a program

Passwords are also needed to protect sensitive and confidential data held on the computer system. This is particularly important in the areas of staff records and also in the case of financial data processed by computer accounting programs.

One solution to the problem of unauthorised employees gaining access to sensitive financial data is the use of **passwords** to gain access to the computer program. Many larger businesses will employ a number of people who need to operate the computer accounting system; they will be issued with an appropriate password. Businesses can also set up **access rights** which restrict certain employees to certain activities and prevent them from accessing more sensitive areas such as the making of payments from the bank account.

When an employee comes to operate, for example, a Sage computer accounting package, he or she will be asked to 'log on'. In the example from Sage Line 50 shown below a person called Tom enters his log on name and a password (CRUISE).

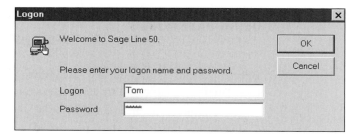

The next screen from Sage Line 50 (see below) shows that Tom and Britney are the two people authorised to access the program. Tom has full access, which means that he can access all the functions of the program. Britney, however, has partial access. She is only allowed to deal with Customers, Suppliers and the Nominal (Main) Ledger. She cannot access the Bank records.

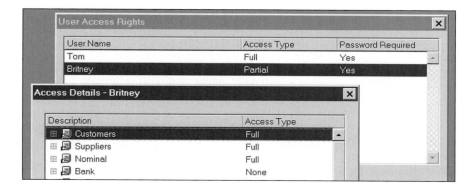

USING SOFTWARE

Using software involves a number of processes with which you should already be familiar.

opening up the program

You should know how to open up the program in the first place, using a password where appropriate (see previous page).

accessing files that you need

The files that you use may be in a familiar folder, or you may have to use a search routine to locate a file, a text document or chart that has been created, or a download from the internet. You need to be tidy in the way that you organise and name files, otherwise you may 'lose' or accidentally overwrite files, in which case you have to go to your back-up (assuming you have made one!)

transferring documents

You should know how to transfer documents from your computer system, to another workstation on the network or as an email attachment to another business – a quotation or copy invoice, for example. There is more on transferring data on the next page.

saving documents

It is critically important to save the data that you input on a frequent and systematic basis (some programs do this automatically). As mentioned above, you should use a logical file naming system when you are saving for the first time and make sure that you know into which folder you have saved a file. There is more on 'saving' on page 26 when we deal with shutting down the computer system.

printing documents

If you use a standalone computer system, the printer will be connected directly to the computer and, as long as it is connected properly, you will be able to print out documents from the 'Print' command. If you use a network you will have to select the printer on-screen and then give the 'Print' command. You may then find that your document will join a print queue and you will then have to locate it when it is printed.

If you are using a computer accounting program you will be able to print out documents such as daybooks, account histories, aged debtor analyses, trial balances, invoices, credit notes and statements.

SAVING, NAMING AND BACKING-UP FILES

During the course of a working day you will need to have a fixed routine for:

- saving and naming files
- backing-up files

saving files

One of the most annoying things about computer operation is to work hard for an extended period of time and then find that you have a power cut, or the computer crashes or that something goes wrong with what you have input. If you have not regularly saved your work, you will lose it.

A routine of regular saving of your work, say every ten minutes or so, will avoid this problem. Some programs help with this, either by saving automatically, or by encouraging you to save by showing a SAVE button after you have completed a task.

Some programs allow you, if you make a mistake, to go back to when you last saved. The more often you save, the less you will have to re-input.

naming files

It is equally important that when you save a new file you allocate it a sensible filename, so that the file can easily be identified. The file should be stored in a suitably named folder so that it can be located quickly. For example, if you are dealing with correspondence with customers you might have a file for each customer:

> A Jones.corres
>
> R Patel.corres
>
> L Smith.corres

These could be stored in a folder named 'Customers'. If you have a large number of customers, you could subdivide the folders into surname groups:

> Customers A-F
>
> Customers G-L
>
> Customers M-R
>
> Customers S-Z

If you are working in an organisation and on a network, there are likely to be conventions for naming files, in which case you should adhere to the convention. If you are working on a computer of your own, you need to be organised and logical when naming files.

backing-up files

You will also need to **back-up** the data generated by the computer. There is no set rule about when you should do this, but it should be at least at the end of every day and preferably when you have completed a long run of inputting.

If you are working on a network,you can normally save to your files, to your work station's hard disk and also to the server. If you have a standalone computer system, the back-up files should be saved to some form of storage device. This may take the form of a disk drive in the workstation itself or it may be an external drive.

Data can be backed up onto a variety of media:

- floppy disks (cheap, traditional but limited in storage capacity)
- Zip disks (higher capacity, higher price)
- tape drive
- writable or rewriteable CDs (cheap and disposable)

Another back-up option is to send files by email and keep them secure at a remote location, although this option would be limited by file size.

back-up policy

It is important that an organisation works out a systematic policy for backup of its data. This should involve:

- backup held on more than one set of disks
- backup disks held off the premises
- periodic backup (eg backups at the end of each month) stored securely

a 'disk per day' back-up system

One solution is for the business to keep a set of floppy disks (or CDs) for each working day labelled with the name of the day and the number of the disk (if there is more than one).

At the end of each working day the data is backed up on the appropriate disk(s), which is (are) kept securely on site. preferably under lock and key.

As a further security measure, a second set of disks could be kept as an off-site back-up. These would be backed up at the end of each day and taken off-site by an employee.

With this system in place the business has double security for its valuable data.

It should also be mentioned that the disks should be replaced periodically (every three months, for example) as they wear out in time and the data can become corrupted.

CLOSE DOWN

Closing down the computer system correctly is important because a variety of problems can arise if the correct procedures are not followed.

When you wish to shut down you should:

• exit each program by using the 'quit' command – this will warn you if you have any unsaved files still open and will enable you to save your work; it will also make sure that the program starts up properly next time the computer is used

• use the correct command from the operating system to close the computer down

If you are using a work station on a network and need to keep the computer turned on – perhaps for someone else to use – you should log off, making sure that all your files are closed, saved and backed up.

GETTING HELP

don't try and fix it yourself unless you know what you are doing!

A computer system that goes wrong can be very frustrating, not only for the organisation, but also for the customers that deal with it. Try booking a holiday at a travel agent when the 'system is down'.

If there is a problem, it should be fixed as soon as possible. If the problem happens to you, and you cannot deal with it yourself, you should know where you can get help.

The type of problems that you are likely to encounter include:

• **hardware** faults – eg a printer that jams, toner that runs out

• **software** faults – program files that corrupt so that the program will not start

• **corrupt data** or **deleted** or **overwritten** data files which stop your normal work flow

hardware failure

There will be times when you have equipment failures. If this happens, the problem should be referred to the person in the organisation who deals with the equipment. It is not advisable to 'have a go' yourself, unless it is a simple matter such as replacing a printer ribbon or cartridge. Many businesses will have back-up computers which can run the software and which can be loaded with your last back-up data disk. There may also be 'on-site' support provided under contract by the supplier of the hardware.

software failure

Software problems can be more complex. If it is a case of not knowing how to carry out a particular operation, refer the matter to someone who does. Help is always at hand through HELP menus, on-line support or telephone technical support to which the business is likely to have subscribed. The rule is again, do not 'have a go' yourself unless you know what you are doing. If a program crashes, it may be necessary to restart the computer. If the program refuses to work after repeated attempts, it may have become corrupted, in which case it may need to be re-installed by a technician.

corrupted, deleted or overwritten data files

Problems can also be caused if a data file you are using

- becomes **corrupt**, ie it becomes unusable and will not open or print, or both
- gets **deleted** by accident when you are tidying up your computer desktop and sending what you think are redundant files into the trash can
- is accidentally **overwritten** by an older version of a file, and in the process wipes out the work you may have done on the file

In these cases you have to rely on your back-up files and hope that they are up-to-date. If you are unable to access them yourself (if, for example, you work on a network) you may need help.

The Case Study that follows illustrates the various problems that can be encountered when running a computer system, and explains the way an employee can overcome those problems.

Case Study

SORTING PROBLEMS

Jo is an accounts assistant at Spira PLC, an insurance company, based in Staines. She works alongside her line manager, Jim Slater.

It is the end of the month and she has been given two tasks to carry out:

1 Printing out all the customer statements ready for mailing.

2 Compiling sales reports for management. These involve inputting sales data into a spreadsheet, extracting charts and pasting them into a word-processing file.

Jo has not been having a very good day at all, and has encountered a number of problems.

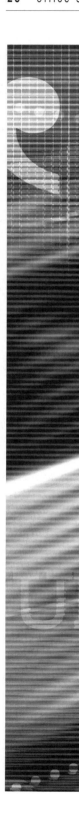

problem 1 – paper out

Jo works on a standalone machine which is used for computer accounting – data input, invoicing and production of reports such as trial balances and aged debtors analyses. The computer has a laser printer linked directly to it for the printing of these documents.

Today Jo has 150 statements of account to print out, fold, place in window envelopes and send out to customers. The statements are generated from a routine in the computer accounting program used by Spira PLC.

When the printer has been running for a while, Jo's computer gives a warning message saying that the printer tray is empty. The 'paper out' light is flashing on the printer.

problem 2 – paper jam

Later in the print run, the printer jams and stops printing. Jo's computer flashes up a warning message and the paper jam light starts flashing on the printer.

problem 3 – a missing file

Jo has been asked to update a sales figures spreadsheet with the figures for the month. She looks in the 'Sales Figures' folder on her hard disk and cannot find the file. She does a 'Search' routine, but the answer comes back 'File not Found'.

problem 4 – software problems

Jo has extracted a chart from a spreadsheet file and needs to export it into a word-processing file as part of a sales report to management. Unfortunately the word-processing file refuses to open when she clicks on it. She then tries to open it through the word-processing file menu, but the program refuses to open. She tries restarting the computer, but still the word-processing program will not start.

The solutions to Jo's problems are as follows:

solution 1 – paper out

Filling up the paper tray on a printer is normally a task most employees would be expected to carry out, as it does not involve any great technical skill. Jo would no doubt be able to replenish the paper supply to enable the printer to complete the statements.

solution 2 – paper jam

Again, most modern printers can easily be opened up so that paper jams can be cleared. If, however, the paper has torn at all, the job may prove more difficult. If this is the case, Jo should report the matter to her line manager so that a technician can be called in to unjam the printer.

solution 3 – a missing file

It would appear that the required file has somehow been accidentally deleted from the computer.

Jo needs to obtain a back-up copy of the file. This should be available in the office. If Jo is not sure where it is located, she should ask her line manager. When the file has been found it should be restored onto the computer so that Jo can resume her work.

solution 4 – software problems

The problem of the faulty software is more serious. it appears that the program files have been corrupted and as a result they do not work.

Jo should report the matter to her line manager who can then arrange for a technician to re-install the program files onto the computer and overwrite the corrupt software. The program files will normally be held in CD form in the office.

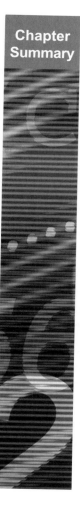

Chapter Summary

- Organisations using computer systems can either use a single standalone machine or a network of computers linked on an intranet. Many computer systems are now linked externally to the internet.

- There is a wide variety of computer programs available – word processing programs, databases, spreadsheets, email managers and computer accounting packages.

- Using computer programs involves a number of processes: opening the program, accessing files, saving, printing. Many programs are written so that you can interchange data from one to another.

- Computer accounting programs combine the functions of a number of different programs – they act as a database and spreadsheet and can generate text and data for use in other programs.

- Visual checks should be made when starting up a computer system. These include checks of hardware and peripherals, power plugs, plugs for peripherals and all cabling.

- Passwords are used for gaining access to data held on a computer system. Passwords are used both for logging on and also for gaining access to different software packages. They can also be used for restricting access to certain types of data.

- Good computer housekeeping involves a strict routine for saving and naming files. It is important to have a consistent back-up policy and ensure that an off-site back up is always maintained.

- A routine for shutting down a computer system should also be established. A system that is not shut down correctly can cause problems when the system is next powered up.

- If problems arise with a computer system, immediate assistance should be sought if the fault cannot be remedied by the employee.

Key Terms

hardware	the computer equipment on which the computer programs run
software	the computer programs which enable the computer to work and carry out its functions
main processing unit	the main computer unit which runs the software
peripheral	an item of hardware – such as an external disk drive or scanner – which is connected to the main processing unit
standalone system	a computer system which is not linked to other computers
network system	a computer system which links a number of computers and shared peripherals – also known as an intranet
internet	a telephone link to an internet service provider giving access to the worldwide web (www)
word processor	a computer program which allows text to be entered and manipulated on screen
database	a computer program which acts as an electronic filing system, storing data so that it can be sorted, searched and organised efficiently
spreadsheet	a computer program which stores text and numbers on a grid system of columns and rows and enables calculations to be performed on the numbers
email management	a program which enables the computer to send and receive emails and to organise messages sent and received
password	a series of letters and/or numbers which are required by the system to enable a computer user to gain access to the system, to software, or certain types of data

Student Activities

1.1 What is the difference between computer hardware and computer software?

1.2 What is the difference between an intranet and the internet?

What are the advantages to an organisation of using an intranet?

1.3 Describe the main functions of the following programs (ie what they 'do'):

(a) a word processing program

(b) a database program

(c) a spreadsheet program

(d) an email management program

(e) a computer accounting program

1.4 You work in the parts department of a local independent garage which runs a standalone computer system to run its accounts and keep records of its stock. The computer is a traditional 'tower' set up with monitor, mouse, keyboard, printer and external zip drive to back-up files at the end of each day.

It is part of your job to operate the computer system, mainly to print invoices for jobs carried out and to check part availability.

Write a numbered checklist of the visual checks to the system you would carry out when you come in the morning, and before you turn the computer on.

1.5 (a) Describe the difference between a system password and a software password.

(b) Explain why the two types of passwords are necessary.

1.6 Give an example of a back-up policy adopted by an organisation. Your source could be an organisation with which you are familiar, information from a friend, or the text in this chapter.

1.7 Computer printers are invaluable when they work well, but can disrupt the work flow when they stop working for one reason or another.

Investigate and list the reasons why a printer might stop working, and in each case state whether the computer operator would be expected to fix the problem, or whether assistance would need to be obtained from elsewhere.

2 Data security

this chapter covers . . .

This chapter explains how data held on computer file is kept secure. Security helps to prevent:

- loss of the data through accidental means, eg disk corruption, viruses
- loss of the data to an unauthorised person, eg someone hacking into the system

Security is maintained through:

- careful use of passwords
- making sure computer hardware and data is located in a safe place
- identifying and dealing with risks to hardware and data

The chapter also deals with the legal regulations relating to the use of computers and the handling of computer data.

NVQ PERFORMANCE CRITERIA COVERED

unit 21: WORKING WITH COMPUTERS

element 21.2

Maintain security of data

A   ensure passwords are kept secret and changed at appropriate times

B   ensure computer hardware and program disks are kept securely located

C   identify potential risks to data from different sources and take steps to resolve or minimise them

D   maintain security and confidentiality of data at all times

E   understand and implement relevant legal regulations

KNOWLEDGE AND UNDERSTANDING COVERAGE

2   the purpose of passwords

6   different types of risk, viruses, confidentiality

7   relevant security and legal regulations, data protection legislation, copyright, VDU legislation, health and safety regulations, retention of documents

12   organisational security policies

INTRODUCTION TO DATA SECURITY

A business that has set up a computer accounting system will have invested thousands of pounds in buying equipment and in training staff to operate it. A business that neglects to look after the equipment and the data that it holds is potentially throwing this money down the drain.

What are the dangers?

dangers to the data

The data held on the computer is irreplaceable once lost and so must be kept securely both on the computer system and also in the form of back ups.

Back-up systems were discussed in the last chapter (page 25). An essential element of data security is the maintenance of a foolproof back-up system and the secure location of back-up disks, both on-site and off-site.

The data must be kept securely to prevent interference from outside and inside the business:

- people such as competitors or criminals outside the business may try to gain access to the data either directly (through 'hacking' if the computer is linked to the internet) or through an employee who can be persuaded to obtain the information

- employees of the business may try to access the data in order to work a fraud – through the payroll, for example, or by making bogus payments to external bank accounts which they control

In this chapter we look at the various precautions that can be taken to minimise these risks.

PASSWORD PROTECTION

We have seen in the last chapter (pages 21-22) that passwords are needed to access:

- the computer system itself (system passwords)
- the software run on the computer system (software passwords)

Security of passwords can be enhanced by individuals choosing 'unbreakable' passwords (see next page).

The organisation can also increase security by ensuring that passwords are changed regularly and when they have been compromised (ie guessed by someone else).

basic rules of choosing an individual password

1   Do not use the word 'password' (it does happen!)

2   Combine letters and numbers if possible.

3   Do not use your own name or date of birth.

4   Make it so that you can remember the password easily and avoid forgettable combinations such as z9ad2w8y7d — try the name and birthday of your first girlfriend/boyfriend, Lisa0511, for example, but avoid using similar details relating to your present partner (because people will guess them).

5   Never write the password down where people can see it, and never put it on a post-it note stuck on the computer monitor (it does happen!)

When you have chosen a password, make sure that nobody stands watching you when you are logging on; the password appears as dots on the screen, but people can work out what you are typing on the keyboard.

If you suspect that someone has worked out your password, change it. If you do not know how to, seek assistance.

organisational procedures for password security

An organisation should ensure that passwords are changed regularly, every couple of months, for example. This will ensure that if an unauthorised person has obtained a password, it can only be used for a limited period.

An organisation should ensure that if there is any suspicion that a password has been 'leaked', there should be a wholesale change of passwords.

IDENTIFYING SECURITY RISKS

Data on computer file needs to be protected against:

*   **corruption** – ie when the file goes 'wrong' and does not work properly – either because of a virus or because of poor storage facilities
*   **loss** – when the file is deleted, accidentally or intentionally – by an employee or by a virus introduced from outside
*   **illegal copying** – by an employee copying a program or by someone 'hacking in' from outside through the internet connection

Clearly the threats to data therefore come both internally, from employees, and externally, from hackers or viruses.

protecting data from internal risks

Much of the data held on computer file is sensitive and confidential in nature, for example:

- payroll details of employees
- financial details relating to customers

It is an unfortunate possibility that employees may be persuaded or paid by outsiders to obtain this information. As a result all employees should take reasonable precautions to prevent data that they are working from being used in this way. For example:

- if you leave your computer, do not leave sensitive data on screen, or the program running
- use a screensaver
- use passwords wherever possible
- if you print out a document with confidential information on it, do not leave it on the printer (or the photocopier!)

Another internal risk is **illegal copying** of computer data – often program files – by employees who 'borrow' disks to take home or 'lend' to friends. The answer here is to keep these types of files under strict control. A business using software will in any event have been granted a **licence** to use it, and any unauthorised copying will be a breach of that licence.

Careful and safe **storage** of computer data on various forms of media is also important. Heat and radiation can damage files held on disk, and the surface of CDs and DVDs can easily be scratched, causing corruption and data loss.

protecting data from external risks

External risks to data include:

- thieves who steal data by stealing the computers on which it is held – computer laptops are particularly vulnerable
- external hackers who access files within an organisation by 'hacking in' from the internet and accessing files held – often on a network
- viruses sent into the computer system, either on a disk or through the internet

Protection against thieves can be achieved by rigorous security at the premises. CCTV is now commonly used to guard against crime. Laptops away from the premises should be kept under lock and key wherever possible, and preferably not left in cars. Hackers can be kept at bay by a 'firewall' on the internet portal of a computer network. A 'firewall' is software which keeps out all external interference and unwanted emails.

Computer viruses are dealt with in the next section.

VIRUS PROTECTION

Computers are vulnerable to viruses. A **virus** is a destructive program which can be introduced into the computer either from a disk or from another computer. If the computer or server which runs the software is linked directly or indirectly to the internet, there is a danger that an incoming email with an attachment may introduce a virus.

Some viruses are relatively harmless and may merely display messages on the screen, others can be very damaging and destroy operating systems and data, putting the computer system completely out of action.

Most computers are now sold already installed with virus protection software which will:

- check for viruses
- destroy known viruses
- check for damage to files on the hard disk
- repair damage to files on the hard disk where possible

This software should be run and updated regularly so that it can deal with the latest viruses.

The screen below shows a virus protection program scanning the hard disk of a computer. As you can see, it has not yet found any infected files.

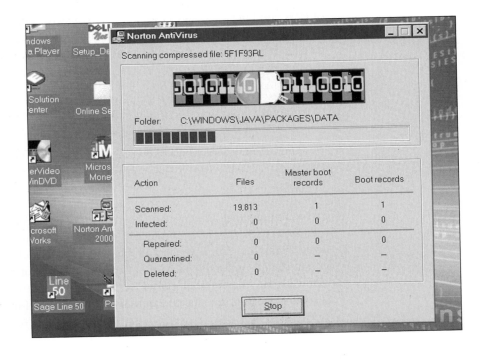

precautions against viruses

There are a number of simple precautions which you can take against viruses:

- be wary of opening any unidentified email attachments which arrive
- use protective software to inspect any disk received from an outside source before opening up any file saved onto it
- make sure that your protective software is up to date – very often they will update automatically over the internet

If your protective software announces that you have a virus, you should report it at once and stop using your computer.

LEGAL REGULATIONS

Any organisation using computer systems must comply with a number of legal requirements.

data protection legislation

Businesses inevitably keep records of their customers and suppliers on file – either manually – a card index system, for example – or, more likely, on computer file. This is 'personal data'.

The **Data Protection Act (1998)** which came into force on 1 March 2000 establishes rules for the processing of personal data. The Act follows the guidelines of an EC Directive and brings the UK in line with European legal principles. The Act applies to a filing system of records held on **computer**, eg a computer database of customer names, addresses, telephone numbers, sales details, or a **manual** set of accessible records.

People have the legal right to know what personal details about them are held by an organisation. They can apply in writing for a copy of the personal data held on file by the organisation; they may have to pay a fee.

We have already seen throughout this book the need for confidentiality in business dealings. The Data Protection Act reinforces this duty. A business should not without permission reveal:

- information about one customer to another customer
- information about its employees

Copyright, Designs and Patents Act,1988

This Act states that it is illegal to copy computer software without the permission of the copyright owner (the writer of the software). This permission is normally granted by **licence**. Software piracy is policed by an independent organisation, FAST (Federation Against Software Theft). A person found copying software is liable to a fine and/or imprisonment!

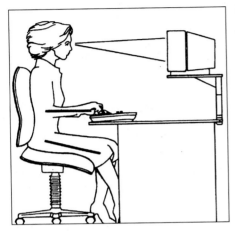

Display Screen Equipment Regulations 1992

These Regulations set down rules for the use of computer workstations and VDU screens. A 'workstation' includes the computer equipment, furniture, space, light and atmosphere in which an employee works. Measures include:

- employees must have regular breaks
- employees must be offered eye tests
- equipment and furniture must conform to strict standards of safety and comfort

If these regulations are not complied with, the employee runs a number of risks, including: a bad back or a bad neck, eye strain, repetitive strain injury and stress.

These regulations apply to the organisation which employs computer operators. It must be remembered, too, that the employee has a responsibility to make sure that regular breaks are taken and that the correct posture is used when working at the computer.

health and safety regulations

The law which governs the overall health and safety issue (including computer systems) is the **Health and Safety at Work Act 1974**. This sets out specific requirements for the employer and employee and is covered in detail in the next chapter.

storing of documents

Business records are normally stored for at least six years (and a minimum of three years for payroll data). The Data Protection Act reinforces the requirement that personal data is kept securely and that it should be accurate. There are a number of legal reasons why financial data (which will include personal data) should be kept for this period of time:

- accounting records should be kept so that they can be inspected by the Inland Revenue if required (if there is a tax inspection)
- accounting records should be kept so that they can be inspected by HM Customs & Excise if required (if there is a VAT inspection)
- accounting records should be kept for at least six years in case they are needed as evidence in any legal action

Chapter Summary

- Passwords restrict access to computer data and are an important aspect of data security. They should be kept secret by the employees that use them.

- The organisation should arrange to change passwords on a regular basis, and should ensure that they are changed after any breach of password security.

- Computer hardware and data (and back-ups) should be stored securely on the premises and in suitable environmental conditions. Any off-site back-ups should also be stored safely.

- Organisations should be aware of the internal risks to data caused by corruption of files, loss and deletion of files and illegal copying.

- Organisations should also be aware of the external risks to data caused by theft, hackers and computer viruses, and take precautions accordingly.

- Confidentiality of data is very important, and data should not be made available without authorisation to outsiders. This is covered under the Data Protection Act.

- Other legislation which affects computer operation includes VDU regulations, rules for the retention of data. and copyright (illegal copying).

Key Terms

password — a collection of letters and/or numbers which give access to a computer system or specific software

corruption — loss of computer data possibly caused by poor storage conditions or a computer virus

illegal copying — unauthorised copying of computer files for personal use – a breach of copyright law

hacker — an individual who breaks into the computer system of an organisation from outside, through an internet connection, to steal or corrupt data

virus — a destructive or disruptive program introduced into a computer system from a disk or concealed in an email attachment

firewall — software which helps protect computer systems connected to the internet

confidentiality of data — keeping computer data secure and preventing unauthorised release to outsiders – covered under the Data Protection Act

Student Activities

2.1   You work in an office which has a networked computer system.

Make up two passwords for your personal use, using a combination of letters and numbers from sources personal to you, eg names, ages, car registrations. The passwords should each have six characters.

Explain in each case why the password can be remembered by you and what the sources of the letters and numbers are. Also state why nobody else could guess them.

Note: do not quote passwords you use at work!

2.2   Assume again that you work in an office which has a networked computer system.

You report directly to a line manager.

Describe what you action you would take in the following circumstances:

(a)   You notice on more than one occasion that a colleague is standing watching you as you input your system password.

(b)   A colleague says to you as you leave work one day, 'Oh, by the way, I am just borrowing this spreadsheet program disk. Remind me to put it back in the morning. It should be OK, nobody seems to mind!'

(c)   You receive an email with an attachment from someone you do not know. The email says 'Open me and be surprised!'

(d)   You are having a heatwave and notice that a colleague has put some floppy disks on the windowsill in full sunlight. They are marked 'on site back-up'.

(e)   A colleague who is very busy inputting data, complains 'My back hurts something terrible when I get home, and my eyes feel really tired all the time. I think I need a change of job.'

(f)   A well-known customer telephones you and asks 'Can you look on screen and let me know if your customer Jaques & Co is paying up on time? We are having trouble getting money out of them at the moment. I hope they are not going bust!' You know from your work that Jaques & Co are very bad at paying their invoices.

Unit 22

Contribute to the maintenance of a healthy, safe and productive working environment

what this unit is about

This unit is about monitoring your working environment and making sure it meets requirements for health, safety, security and effective working conditions. You must show that you can achieve this standard of health, safety and security in all areas of your work.

The Unit is dealt with by four chapters which cover the two elements:

Element 22.1	Chapter 3	**Who is responsible for health and safety?**
	Chapter 4	**Who deals with the hazards?**
	Chapter 5	**Accidents and emergencies**
Element 22.2	Chapter 6	**Managing your work area**

Who is responsible for health and safety?

It is easy to state the obvious fact that an employee needs a healthy, safe and secure workplace. It is less easy to decide who is responsible for that level of health, safety and security – the employer or the employee?

This chapter examines:

- *the hazards and risks encountered in the workplace*

- *what the law says about the responsibility of the employer and the employee*

- *some of the paperwork that the law requires the employer to complete*

NVQ PERFORMANCE CRITERIA COVERED

unit 22:   CONTRIBUTE TO THE MAINTENANCE OF A HEALTHY, SAFE AND PRODUCTIVE WORKING ENVIRONMENT

element 22.1

Monitor and maintain a safe, healthy and secure working environment

A   *make sure you read, comply with and have up-to-date information on the health, safety and security requirements and procedures for your workplace*

KNOWLEDGE AND UNDERSTANDING COVERAGE

1   *the importance of health, safety and security in your workplace*

2   *the basic requirements of the health and safety and other legislation and regulations that apply to your workplace*

3   *the person(s) responsible for health, safety and security in your workplace*

4   *the relevant up-to-date information on health, safety and security that applies to your workplace*

HEALTH, SAFETY AND SECURITY

This Unit requires you to understand the need for health, safety and security in the workplace. Both the employee and the employer have responsibilities for maintaining a reasonable level of health, safety and security.

health

All employees need to be healthy to work efficiently. If you are suffering from malaria or have three broken ribs, your performance is likely to suffer.

Sometimes ill health can be your own fault. If you eat a dodgy curry, drink twelve pints of lager at lunchtime or go bungee jumping you may well be asking for trouble.

On the other hand, if you are required to sit in front of a VDU for six hours at a stretch, or the heating is turned down so low in the depths of winter that your fingers turn blue and you catch a cold, your employer is likely to be at fault.

safety

Employees and employers also need to be aware of safety in the workplace. Of course, some places of employment are more obviously dangerous than others.

If you work on a building site or on a production line, you need to take great care of your personal safety, and so does your employer.

If you work in an office, you will need to take care when operating equipment such as a guillotine (which has a very sharp blade) and your employer will also need to make sure that the metal guard for the guillotine is always in place to prevent loss of fingers.

security

Security means keeping the workplace and employees free from intrusion from outsiders and also from unauthorised employees. Threats include:
- theft of business equipment such as computers and vehicles
- theft of money and valuables owned by employees
- theft of business information held on computer and paper files
- damage to equipment
- harassment of individuals

Remember that both employees and employers are responsible for security and that breaches of security can come from employees as well.

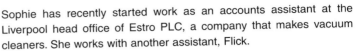

Case Study

WHOSE FAULT IS IT?

Sophie has recently started work as an accounts assistant at the Liverpool head office of Estro PLC, a company that makes vacuum cleaners. She works with another assistant, Flick.

During the course of a working day Sophie encounters a number of issues which relate to health, safety and security.

See if you can identify the problems, decide who is responsible and realise what could happen as a result of the situation. Then read the suggested solution on the next page.

situation 1 – Sophie trips up   SAFETY

Sophie was walking around Flick's desk when she tripped up over an electric lead. After she had picked herself up Flick apologised: 'Sorry. I was just charging up my laptop and the only free socket I could find for the charger was just across the room!'   FLICK - FAULT
SOPHIE SHOULD PAY ATTENTION. —MORE SOCKETS

situation 2 – Sophie finds the petty cash tin

Sophie had to go to the supervisor's desk and noticed that the petty cash tin was sitting on the top of the desk. It was unlocked and Nora the supervisor was not there. The petty cash tin is officially under the supervisor's control.
SECURITY   SOPHIE SHOULD lock CASE + find SUPERVISOR .

situation 3 – Sophie gets eyestrain

Sophie complained to Flick that she was getting eyestrain and headaches: 'I have to do invoicing on this computer hour after hour, inputting details from purchase orders. It is really boring. They never give a break because we are so busy.'
Employer should give designated breaks / Sophie should take breaks

situation 4 – Flick forgets her password

Flick had a bad memory and could never remember the password which she needed to get into the accounts program on the company's networked computers. She decided to write it down on a 'Post-it' note and stick it on the side of her VDU screen. 'Is that a good idea?' asked Sophie. 'No problem,' replied Flick.   YES Security problem
Flick is wrong + Sophie should be in the...

situation 5 – Flick drops her soup

Flick was having a bad day. She dropped her cuppa soup on the lino kitchen floor. 'I'll clear it up in a minute,' she said and went off to make a telephone call.
CLEAN up STRAIGHT AWAY.

situation 6 – Sophie goes for a smoke

Sophie was trying to give up smoking, but was not doing too well, even though the office was a no smoking zone. She was outside having a smoke with a colleague when she noticed that the despatch department had put a pallet of packages just outside the office fire escape door. 'Hope we don't have a fire today,' she muttered to her friend.
NOTE + MOVE THE OBSTRUCTION

solutions

There is not always a set solution to every problem, but an experienced colleague might have explained the situations to Sophie and Flick as follows:

situation 1 – Sophie trips up

Flick is at fault here because she has trailed the wire across the room and tripped up Sophie. She admits the fault by apologising. Her workplace supervisor should have stopped her doing this if she had realised what was going on. The result of the accident could be an injury to Sophie which could keep her off work.

situation 2 – Sophie finds the petty cash tin

Petty cash should always be kept under lock and key. The supervisor is responsible for the cash, even if she is away from her desk. Either she has left the cash out unlocked, or someone else has helped themselves. Security has been breached and the supervisor is responsible for what has happened.

situation 3 – Sophie gets eyestrain

Sophie has been made to sit in front of the computer and input invoices. Eyestrain and headaches are common symptoms in people who do not take regular breaks from inputting. The employer is at fault here. The end result could be a deterioration in Sophie's health and even a case of RSI (Repetitive Strain Injury).

situation 4 – Flick forgets her password

Passwords are used as security devices on computers to prevent outsiders and unauthorised employees gaining access to information. If Flick displays her password for the whole office to see she is breaching security and risking the company's accounting data.

situation 5 – Flick drops her soup

Flick was certainly having a bad day. Her cuppa soup on the lino kitchen floor is a safety hazard because anyone coming into the kitchen could slip on the soup, fall over and injure themselves. The fact that Flick has gone off to make a telephone call shows that she does not think a lot about her colleagues' safety.

situation 6 – Sophie goes for a smoke

Sophie is not helping her health by smoking, but at least she is observing the No Smoking restrictions in the workplace. She is right to point out the hazard of the pallet of packages just outside the fire escape door.

If there had been a fire, the exit would have been blocked and the result could have been loss of life. The responsibility here lies with the despatch department. As the department is under the control of the company, in the event of a fire the company would have been held responsible. In this case it would also have been Sophie's duty to alert the despatch department to the hazard.

HAZARDS AND RISKS

The Case Study on the last two pages has used the terms **hazards** and **risks**. What is the difference between 'hazards' and 'risks'? In any study of health and safety it is important to distinguish between the two.

A **hazard** *is something that could cause you harm.*

A **risk** *measures how likely it is that the hazard will harm you.*

For example, if you are working on a building site, the hazards you face when walking along a high steel beam are:

- you could lose concentration and fall off
- someone could drop a hammer which could hit you and knock you off
- you could be struck by lightning

These are all hazards, but the risks attached to them vary. The risk of being struck by lightning, for example, is likely to be lower than that of falling off the beam through lack of concentration.

When you are examining health and safety in the workplace it is important that you:

hazards are things that can harm you

- **identify** hazards
- **assess** risks

Taking the building site example, the employer is likely to supply the employee with a safety harness, but is less likely to provide him with a lightning conductor, because the risk of being struck by lightning will be less. We will look at the need for an employer to undertake a **risk assessment** later in this book (page 61).

hazards and risks: some facts . . .

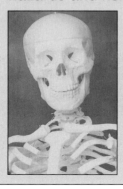

- one in every 100,000 workers is likely to be killed at work every year
- 650 in every 100,000 workers is likely to be injured at work every year
- the most common forms of accident at work are: falling from a height, being struck by a moving vehicle, being struck by moving or falling objects
- rates of fatal and non-fatal injury are higher in men than in women
- rates of fatal injury are highest for older male workers
- the rate of less serious injury is higher in young men compared with older men

Source: Health & Safety Statistics from www.hse.gov.uk

HEALTH AND SAFETY LAW

We have already seen in the Case Study earlier in the chapter that responsibility for health, safety and security in the workplace rests both with the employee and the employer. This is common sense. But when there is an incident and a dispute over the incident – for example, someone injured by equipment when they should have been wearing protective gloves – common sense is sometimes forgotten. This is where the law becomes important because it lays down a structure of regulations in the workplace:

- to ensure that health and safety measures are introduced and observed both by employers and employees
- to specify the rights and responsibilities of employers and employees
- to enable employees to obtain compensation in the case of injury or ill health caused by conditions in the workplace

HEALTH AND SAFETY AT WORK ACT 1974

The main Act of Parliament which governs health and safety is the **Health and Safety at Work Act 1974**. This not only sets out specific requirements for the employer and employee (see below), but also allows further rules to be established in the form of Regulations, Codes of Practice and Guidance.

to whom does the Act apply?

The Health and Safety at Work Act covers:

- all work premises of any type and size
- employees and employers
- business visitors
- people and businesses brought onto the premises and employed to carry out specific tasks, eg photocopier servicing, sandwich deliveries
- members of the public who happen to call

duties of employers

The Health and Safety at Work Act requires that employers must 'as far as is reasonably practicable':

1 Ensure the health, safety and welfare at work of employees, including:
   - the maintenance of safe entry and exit routes
   - providing a safe working environment
   - providing well-maintained and safe equipment

- storing articles and substances safely

- providing protective clothing where appropriate

- providing information about safety in the workplace

- providing appropriate training and supervision

2   Prepare and continually update a written statement of the health and safety policy of the organisation – the **Health and Safety Policy Statement**. This requirement applies to organisations of five or more employees. The employer must make sure that the policy statement is circulated to all employees.

3   Allow for the appointment of union members as **safety representatives** who must be allowed to:

- investigate accidents

- investigate potential hazards

- follow up employee complaints

- have paid time off to carry out their duties

duties of employees

The Health and Safety at Work Act requires that all employees must:

- take reasonable care of their own health and safety

- take reasonable care of the health and safety of others who might be affected by their actions

- cooperate with the employer and anyone acting on his or her behalf to meet health and safety requirements

OTHER HEALTH AND SAFETY LEGISLATION

You will be relieved to hear that you are not required in your studies to memorise the names of all the laws, Directives, Regulations and Codes of Practice that supplement the Health and Safety at Work Act and protect employees in the workplace. You must, however, be aware of their existence and the impact they have on the way in which the workplace is regulated. These include:

Workplace (Health, Safety and Welfare) Regulations 1992

These complement the Health and Safety at Work Act and regulate safety, cleanliness and the workplace environment.

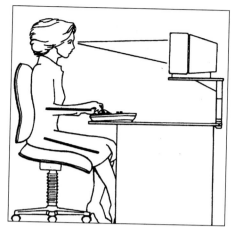

Display Screen Equipment Regulations 1992

These Regulations set down rules for the use of computer workstations and VDU screens. A 'workstation' includes the computer equipment, furniture, space, light and atmosphere in which an employee works. Measures include:

- employees must have regular breaks

- employees must be offered eye tests

- equipment and furniture must conform to strict standards of safety and comfort

Control of Substances Hazardous to Health 1999

Hazardous substances must be identified and stored in a safe manner. Employees dealing with a hazardous substance – whether it is radioactive waste or bleach – must be supplied with and wear suitable protective clothing. The 'Control of Substances Hazardous to Health' is often abbreviated to 'COSHH'.

Reporting of Injuries, Diseases and Dangerous Occurrences Regulations 1995 (RIDDOR)

These regulations require that the Health and Safety Executive (a Government agency) must be notified on official RIDDOR forms of fatal or serious injuries, dangerous occurrences or serious diseases in the workplace. See page 69 for further details of the requirements of these regulations.

other regulations

There are other regulations, the purposes of which are self-explanatory:

- Fire Precautions Regulations

- Electricity at Work Regulations

- Noise at Work Regulations

- Health and Safety (First Aid) Regulations

- Health and Safety (Safety Signs and Signals) Regulations

- Employer's Liability (Compulsory Insurance) Regulations

So that you can appreciate the extent of all these laws and regulations, you should read the Health and Safety 'checklist for office workers' our authors have compiled and which is shown on the next page. This sets out the most important office-based health and safety obligations of employers.

EMPLOYER HEALTH AND SAFETY CHECKLIST

an employer's duties to office employees

1   The workplace should allow at least $3.715m^2$ of floor space and at least 11 cubic metres of space to each employee.

2   The temperature of the office should be not less than 16°C after the first hour of work.

3   The office should be effectively ventilated by fresh or purified air.

4   There must be adequate natural or artificial light.

5   The office must be cleaned regularly and frequently, and rubbish cleared away.

6   There should be sufficient toilet and washing facilities.

7   Drinking water (tap or fountain) must be made available.

8   Rest areas with adequate seating must be provided.

9   Employees must have the facilities so that they can eat on the premises.

10   Employees must be able to hang up outdoor clothing in the office.

11   There must be first aid facilities for employees – normally in the shape of a trained first aider and a first aid box.

12   There must be fire fighting equipment available and adequately signed escape routes.

13   Office equipment and machinery must be adequately maintained, and employees protected from any device which could be dangerous.

14   Doors and floors and windows must be safe.

15   Employees must be able to move around the workplace freely and without obstruction.

16   Safety rails and other safeguards must be installed in places where there is a risk of employees falling from a height.

17   Employees must be asked to read the organisation's Health and Safety Policy Statement (organisations with five or more employees).

18   Employees must be told where the accident book is.

19   Employees must be told where the Health and Safety 'poster' is situated.

20   Employees must be told about emergency and evacuation procedures.

POLICING HEALTH AND SAFETY

There are two public sector regulatory bodies that oversee Health and Safety law and regulations:

- **Health and Safety Commission** – which has overall responsibility for research, training, health and safety information provision and the drafting of Regulations and Codes of Practice
- **Health and Safety Executive (HSE)** – which puts Health and Safety controls into practice, employing lawyers, specialists and inspectors and Local Authorities to oversee and 'police' the implementation of the various regulations

Visit www.hse.gov.uk for further details:

the law in action

The **Health and Safety Executive** employs its own inspectors to visit premises, and Local Authorities employ environmental health officers to inspect shops and offices. If unsatisfactory working conditions are found an **improvement notice** may be issued. If conditions are irretrievably bad a **prohibition notice** may be issued, the faulty equipment will have to be shut down and the owner may face prosecution. (Fawlty Towers fans may remember the episode of the rat!) Do not forget that an **employee** also has obligations under Health and Safety regulations and may be prosecuted and fined in extreme circumstances for breaches of the regulations.

HEALTH AND SAFETY REQUIREMENTS IN THE WORKPLACE

The first performance criterion of Unit 22 Element 1 is that you should:

'make sure you read, comply with and have up-to-date information on the health, safety and security requirements and procedures for your workplace.'

We will now explain where you should be able to find this information.

Health and Safety Policy Statement

The law requires that every employer who employs five or more employees must draw up a written **Health and Safety Policy Statement**. This

document must be shown to every employee who then has a duty to study it. Most employers will obtain each employee's signature on a form saying that they have read the Statement. The document includes:

- the names of the people responsible for health and safety

- arrangements for: risk assessment, employee consultation, safety when operating machinery, handling of unsafe substances, information, training, accident reporting, illness reporting

- emergency procedures

- forms for reporting accidents and hazards

the Health and Safety 'poster'

Employers are also required to display a poster produced by the Health and Safety Executive, or provide an approved leaflet which summarises the employer's obligations (see below). These are very useful documents for summarising much of what has been said in this chapter.

emergency procedures

Employees should be familiar with the emergency procedures for events such as fires and bomb threats, when they will have to evacuate the building. These situations are covered in more detail in Chapter 5 'Accidents and emergencies'.

the accident book

Employees should also be familiar with the 'accident book'. This is a record of accidents which occur in the workplace and should be completed each time there is some form of mishap. Employers often have a trained 'first aider' on the staff who will be able to treat accidents and injuries. Serious accidents involving death, amputation, loss of sight, explosions and building collapse should be reported immediately to the appropriate Local Authority.

These 'A & E' situations are also covered in more detail in Chapter 5 'Accidents and emergencies'.

the Health and Safety Officer

Most employers will have a Health and Safety Officer on the payroll. This may be a union member, or if there is no union representation in the workplace, an employee appointed to look after health and safety matters. The name of this representative will normally be written on the 'Health and Safety Poster'. Employees should make it their business to find out who this person is. If there is a health and safety problem, the representative will need to be consulted.

Chapter Summary

- Both employer and employees have responsibility for health, safety and security in the workplace.

- The employer is responsible for identifying hazards in the workplace and assessing the risk elements involved in those hazards. The employer should take appropriate action to protect employees against the hazards.

- The responsibilities of employer and employee are set out in the Health and Safety at Work Act and other legislation, Directives, Regulations and Codes of Practice. These cover a wide variety of hazards, including exposure to VDUs, dangerous substances, disease, fire, electricity and noise.

- The Government bodies responsible for health and safety in the workplace are the Health and Safety Commission (which establishes health and safety control principles) and the Health and Safety Executive (which puts the principles into practice with the help of the Local Authority).

- Health and Safety information in the workplace may be found in the Health and Safety Policy Statement, on the Health and Safety poster, in the various emergency procedures and from a Health and Safety Representative.

Key Terms		
hazard	something that could cause you harm
risk	measurement of how likely it is that you will be harmed by a hazard
risk assessment	formal assessment by an employer of the hazards and risks in the workplace
safety officer	a person (who may be a union member) appointed to investigate health and safety problems and accidents in the workplace
Health and Safety Commission	Government body which has overall responsibility for drafting of health and safety regulations for the workplace
Health and Safety Executive (HSE)	Government body which puts health and safety controls into operation with the help of the Local Authorities
improvement notice	a notice issued by an HSE inspector or local environmental health officer requiring the improvement of unsatisfactory workplace conditions
prohibition notice	a notice issued by an HSE inspector or local environmental health officer requiring the closure of unsatisfactory workplace conditions
Health and Safety Policy Statement	a document required by law stating how an employer deals with health and safety issues in the workplace
accident book	a record of workplace accidents

Student Activities

3.1   Who is responsible for the maintenance of a healthy, safe and secure working environment?

Both Employee + Employer.

3.2   What is the difference between a hazard and a risk?

Hazard — Could could harm / Risk — How likely you are to be harmed

3.3   (a)   What is the main Act which regulates health and safety in the workplace?

H+S ACT 1974

     (b)   Give three examples of the duties of an employer under this Act

Good working environment / Good ventilation / comfortable work temperature.

     (c)   Give three examples of the duties of an employee under this Act

Reasonable care of their own H&S.

Think of work colleguss H+S.

Cooperat with the H+S Requirements at work.

3.4   What do the following abbreviations stand for? Explain what they are.

(a)   COSHH   *control of substances Hazardous to health*

(b)   RIDDOR   *— Report of Injury, Disease + Dangerous occurrence's Regulations.*

(c)   HSE   *— Health + Safety Executive.*

3.5   What is the main document drawn up by an employer which tells employees about health and safety in the workplace? Choose one from the following:

(a)   Health and Safety Executive Statement *?*

(b)   Health and Safety Policy Statement   ✓

(c)   Accident book

(d)   Incident book

3.6   Study the pictures shown below. What hazards can you identify? State in each case whether the hazard is the responsibility of the employer or the employee.

(a)

Hazard
Employer

(b)

Hazard
Employee

(c)

Employer
Employee.

(d)

Employee.

this chapter covers . . .

In the last chapter we examined the responsibilities of the employer and employee for health and safety in the workplace. We also outlined some of the legislation that regulates health and safety. In this chapter we examine some of the health and safety hazards – and how they are dealt with – in more detail. This chapter explains:

- the common types of health, safety and security hazards

- hazards you can put right yourself and hazards that you need to report

- the ways in which an employer will assess risks in the workplace

NVQ PERFORMANCE CRITERIA COVERED

unit 22:   CONTRIBUTE TO THE MAINTENANCE OF A HEALTHY, SAFE AND PRODUCTIVE WORKING ENVIRONMENT

element 22.1

Monitor and maintain a safe, healthy and secure working environment

A   make sure you read, comply with and have up-to-date information on the health, safety and security requirements and procedures for your workplace

B   make sure that the procedures are being followed and report any that are not to the relevant person

C   identify and correct any hazards that you can deal with safely, competently and within the limits of your authority

D   promptly and accurately report any hazards that you are not allowed to deal with to the relevant person and warn other people who may be affected

F   identify and recommend opportunities for improving health, safety and security to the responsible person

KNOWLEDGE AND UNDERSTANDING COVERAGE

5   the importance of being alert to health, safety and security hazards

6   the common health, safety and security hazards that affect people working in an administrative role and how to identify these

7   hazards you can put right yourself and hazards you must report

8   the importance of warning others about hazards and how to do so until the hazard is dealt with

11   how to recommend improvements to health and safety

TYPES OF HAZARD

The type of hazard you will encounter depends on your working environment. The last chapter looked briefly at the types of hazard encountered on a building site to emphasise the fact that not everybody works in an office. Being an office worker is clearly safer than being a lumberjack or a fire fighter, and in view of the fact that most readers of this book will work in an office, we will focus on office hazards in this chapter.

Hazards are generally:

• health and safety hazards, or

• security hazards

health and safety hazards

Most accidents and hazards to health result from the following:

• poor flooring – slippery floors, uneven floors, frayed carpets

• electrical problems – trailing leads and cables, frayed and bare wires

• blockages and obstacles to progress – filing drawers left open, waste bins in the way, boxes stacked up in corridors

• fire doors wedged open (ie safety doors that normally swing shut)

• employees taking gymnastic risks – standing on chairs and desks, lifting items that are too heavy or not bending properly when lifting

• employees getting too excited – running around the office, playing practical jokes, tripping people up

• using harmful substances without wearing protective clothing – for example pouring bleach down a blocked toilet and not wearing gloves

• using a computer workstation and not taking regular breaks or not using suitable seating

security hazards

Security hazards can take a number of different forms:

• money left lying around

• confidential records left lying around (the photocopier is a favourite place)

• passwords on Post-it notes on computer screens

• visitors left unattended

• strangers wandering around the office pretending to be computer engineers and 'borrowing' the equipment

• exterior doors left unattended or unlocked – particularly where there is valuable equipment, money or sensitive information in the office

The problem with these hazards is knowing when you can deal with them and realising when you have to tell someone else in the organisation about them. The Case Study that follows illustrates this.

SOPHIE'S CHOICE

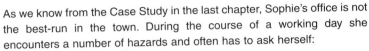

As we know from the Case Study in the last chapter, Sophie's office is not the best-run in the town. During the course of a working day she encounters a number of hazards and often has to ask herself:

'Do I deal with this, or do I need to let someone else know that there is a problem?'

What do you think Sophie should do in each of the following situations?

situation 1 – the filing cabinet drawer

Sophie walked into the section where the customer files were kept and tripped up over an open filing cabinet drawer. She hurt her leg a bit, but there was no injury. *ACCIDENT BK*
SHUT DRAW

situation 2 – problems with the photocopier

The photocopier in the office has a paper jam. Sophie knows that opening up the copier is relatively simple – as she has done it before – but it can be messy. She is wearing a new white shirt and is worried about getting the toner on her clothes. *SWITCH OFF — REMOVE JAM*

situation 3 – more problems with the photocopier

Sophie notices that the power supply cable to the photocopier is wrapped around the wheel on the base of the machine and is getting worn. *TURN OFF + PUT A SIGN ON IT. + Inform Someone & GET AN ELECTRICIAN TO REPLACE CABLE*

situation 4 – problems with the ventilation

It is July and the office is getting very hot. 'Why don't you open that window, Soph?' asks Flick. 'You can easily reach it if you stand on that chair!'

'I am not too good at heights!' says Sophie. *GET SOMEONE TO OPEN IT FOR HER/IF SHE DOES WINDOW THEN GET SUPPORT*

situation 5 – problems with the window

Sophie notices that the window has a broken lock on it. *REPORT TO SUPERVISOR — SAFETY BREECH. — AW HE—*

situation 6 – the engineer calls

A stranger walks into the office and starts fiddling with one of the new computers they have just had installed. 'Can I help you at all?' asks Sophie.

'No. I'm OK, thank you. I think I am going to have to take this one away back to the workshop to check the hard drive.' *CHECK I.D FOR ENGINEER. REPORT TO SOMEONE AS A SAFETY BREECH.*

solutions

As with the Case Study in the last chapter, there is not always a clear cut solution to every problem, but it is likely that Sophie will react as follows:

situation 1 – the filing cabinet drawer

Sophie has walked straight into a common office hazard and hurt herself. There is no need to involve anyone else as she is not injured and she will not need to record anything in the accident book. All she needs to do is to shut the drawer. If she finds out who has left the drawer open, she could, of course, let that person know what she thinks of them.

situation 2 – problems with the photocopier — *Bollocks*

The photocopier with a paper jam is a common problem and is often accompanied by the potential hazard of being covered in black powder. Sophie just needs to take care when replacing the toner, or she could ask someone else nicely if they would do it for her. There is certainly no need to refer the matter to anyone else.

Sophie reports the problems

situation 3 – more problems with the photocopier

The worn power supply cable to the photocopier is certainly a risk and needs to be referred to a supervisor or manager as soon as possible. If it is not seen to, the worn cable could start a fire or electrocute someone.

situation 4 – problems with the ventilation

Poor ventilation in summer is a common problem. The employer has a duty to provide adequate ventilation and Sophie is quite at liberty to open the window if she wants to. She will need to take care when opening it, and it is her responsibility to make sure that she does not take undue risks, such as standing on a chair. Only if the window is beyond any employee's reach should the employer be asked to arrange for it to be opened.

situation 5 – problems with the window

A broken lock is a serious security risk. Sophie must tell her employer about it as soon as possible so that it can be replaced.

situation 6 – the engineer calls

It can often be easy for intruders to gain access to offices and to walk off with valuable equipment. It is Sophie's responsibility here to establish the identity of the person, and if in any doubt to contact 'Security' to deal with the intruder.

REPORTING HAZARDS

The Case Study on the last two pages has shown that it is not good enough just to identify hazards to health, safety and security in the workplace. They have to be dealt with or reported.

It is also important to warn other people in the workplace of the dangers of hazards. The Case Study that follows shows what an employee should do when a hazard is identified.

SOPHIE'S FALL

Sophie's office has recently been extended and a new room has been added. The extension is at a slightly lower level than the old office and so going into the new area involves going down a low step where the door is.

One or two people have not noticed this drop in level and have stumbled, spilt coffee and generally been annoyed because there has been no warning notice on the door. But nobody had done anything about it.

Today Sophie was carrying a pile of files which were being transfered to the new office. She went through the new door, stumbled and dropped all the files on the floor. The papers spilled out and the air went quite blue for a while. Sophie was unhurt but very annoyed.

'I am going to do something about this. I seem to be the only person around here who is capable of doing anything!'

Sophie decided to write out a temporary notice to stick on the door straightaway:

> # Mind the step!

She also wrote a memo to Guido, the Office Manager:

Memorandum

From: Sophie Weston, Accounts Assistant

To: Guido Manzini, Office Manager　　　　　　　Date: 28 November 2003

Subject: Safety Hazards

This is to let you know that the step between the old office and the new extension is becoming a safety hazard. A number of people have stumbled, not knowing the step is there. I am concerned that someone, either an employee or a visitor, will be injured. I have stuck up a temporary warning notice, but recommend that action is taken soon.

RISK ASSESSMENT BY THE EMPLOYER

So far in this chapter we have examined issues of health, safety and security mostly from the employee's point of view – dealing with questions such 'what do I need to deal with . . . what do I need to report to my employer?' But it is important to appreciate that the main burden of identifying hazards and assessing risks lies with the employer. The law states that an employer should carry out a **risk assessment**.

what is a risk assessment?

A risk assessment is a careful examination by the employer of what could cause harm to people in the workplace or cause them to become ill.

The risk assessment is a written document prepared by the employer, often incorporated into the Health and Safety Policy Statement.

The main objectives for an employer drawing up a risk assessment are to:

- decide whether a **hazard** (something that can cause harm) is significant
- ensure that if it is significant, there are adequate precautions in place to minimise the **risk** to the employee or any other person on the premises

some risks to assess

For example if there is machinery to operate, the operator should be kept well away from moving parts and wear protective clothing. On a more domestic level, if there is bleach in the company kitchen, any one using it should be told to wear gloves. It all really comes down to common sense.

The Health and Safety Executive publishes useful downloadable free leaflets on www.hse.gov.uk The main HSE document is 'Five steps to Risk Assessment'. The five steps are:

Step 1: Look for the hazards.
As an employee you may well be consulted when your employer looks for hazards. You may be asked directly, or your union rep may be asked.

Step 2: Decide who might be harmed, and how.
This will include employees, cleaners, visitors, contractors, and members of the public. Special attention should be paid to new employees and pregnant employees, for obvious reasons.

Step 3: Evaluate the risks and decide whether the existing precautions are adequate or whether more should be done.
Risks can be high, medium or low. They should be made low if at all possible. Again, common sense should prevail.

Step 4: Record your findings.

This is only necessary if there are five or more employees. The findings should be written down and employees should be asked to read them. New recruits are normally asked to read them when they join. The record of findings should show that a proper check was made, employees were consulted, the hazards identified and precautions put into place which makes the risk a low one.

Step 5: Review your assessment and revise it if necessary.

Organisations are always changing, and so will the hazards and risks. The risk assessment should therefore be reviewed on a regular basis.

Illustrated below is a typical risk assessment for bleach, a substance classed as hazardous under the COSHH (Control of Substances Hazardous to Health) Regulations and found on most premises.

COSHH SHEET

BLEACH

Hazard class:	Hazardous
Handling:	Irritant to eyes and skin. Use protective gloves.
If spillage occurs:	Wash away with water.
Recommendation:	Keep stored away safely.
Conclusion:	To be handled with care.
Indication of risk:	Irritant to eyes/skin.
First Aid:	In case of contact with eyes, hold eye open, rinse with plenty of water and seek medical advice.
	If swallowed do not induce vomiting. Give small sips of water.
	Seek medical advice.
	If spilt on clothes, remove any contaminated clothing and wash skin with soap and water.

---

taking further action

If the employer seems to ignore health and safety legal requirements, employees (or their union reps) have the right to take the matter to the Local Authority and HSE. These bodies can send in inspectors and have power to enforce the law. They can also advise employers and employees on a more friendly basis if they have health and safety queries.

Chapter Summary

- There are always likely to be hazards to health, safety and security, whatever the working environment – building site or office.

- Health and safety hazards in an office often relate to the physical environment: floors, doors, furniture, passageways, electrical equipment. They also relate to the people in the workplace not taking care and behaving badly.

- Security hazards involve threats from outsiders and also from employees. Security hazards relate to valuables – money, machines, data – being treated negligently by employees and being stolen by outsiders.

- Employees who have to deal with hazards in the workplace should be able to decide whether to deal with the hazards themselves or whether to report them to another person. This decision will obviously depend on the hazard.

- When an employee identifies a hazard, there may be a need both to report it and to warn other employees about it.

- It is a legal requirement for an employer to carry out a risk assessment by identifying hazards, assessing the level of risk and taking the necessary precautions.

Key Terms

hazard	something that could cause you harm
risk	the extent to which a hazard can harm someone
health hazard	a hazard in the workplace which can damage the health of employees – it can take the form of a substance (including air quality), noise, and radiation from VDUs
safety hazard	a physical hazard in the workplace which can cause an accident
security hazard	a hazard in the workplace which can result in intrusion, either by an employee or by an outsider
risk assessment	a formal document, required by law, identifying hazards in the workplace and establishing precautions to minimise risk

Student Activities

The next two activities are based around a series of situations which you might encounter in the workplace. Consider the situations in turn and:

- **identify each hazard**

- **consider what you would do about it by choosing one of the given options, giving your reasons in each case**

4.1 You hear the fire alarm going off. It is Friday and the fire drills are often held on a Friday. One of your colleagues says she has to back up her computer data as she has just done a long run of invoices. 'I don't want to lose that lot!' she says.

The employees assemble as usual outside in the car park. The names are read out and your colleague is not there. Do you say:

(a) 'I think she has just gone to the loo.'

(b) 'She is just backing up her computer data ~~and will be out here soon.~~'

(c) Nothing.

Give your reasons. *BOLLOCK HER .*
KNOW WHERE TO LOOK /
IF BAD FIRE .

4.2 You notice that a colleague who processes the company payroll (which is password protected) is always leaving his computer on during his lunch hour. As a result, anyone passing by can access data about employees' pay and obtain other personal details.

Do you:

(a) Ignore the situation.

(b) Go up to your colleague just as he is leaving for lunch and politely suggest that he logs off the payroll data in case anybody sees it. *※*

(c) Tell your line manager about the situation. *※*

Give your reasons. *DATA PROTECTION ACT , BANK DETAILS SHOWING .*
AMEND PAYROLL — SECURITY BREACH

The third activity involves the use of a VDU (computer screen) which is sometimes thought to be a health hazard in the workplace.

4.3 You have been given a HSE leaflet 'Working with VDUs' by your Union rep. This covers the Display Screen Equipment Regulations and can also be downloaded from www.hse.gov.uk as a free leaflet.

Here are some extracts from the leaflet:

'. . . *only a small proportion of VDU users actually suffer ill health as a result of their work. Where problems do occur, they are generally caused by the way in which the VDUs are being used, rather than the VDUs themselves.*'

'Some users may get aches and pains in their hands, wrists, arms, neck, shoulders or back, especially after long periods of uninterrupted VDU work . . . Problems of this kind may have a physical cause, but may also be more likely if a VDU user feels stressed by the work.'

'Extensive research has found no evidence that VDUs can cause disease or permanent damage to the eyes. But long spells of VDU work can lead to tired eyes and discomfort.'

'Headaches may result from several things that occur with VDU work such as:

- screen glare
- poor image quality
- a need for different spectacles
- stress from the pace of work
- anxiety about new technology
- reading the screen for long periods without a break
- poor posture, or
- a combination of these'

The leaflet also states that employers have a legal duty to provide adjustable chairs, a footrest if required, adequate lighting (but no glare) and sufficient desk space.

The display screens should be clear, non-reflective and adjustable.

Employees should be given suitable training and regular breaks when working.

the situation

Trish (see picture below) uses the computer to process sales orders most of the day.

She complains that she is getting aches and pains in her neck and arms and also bad headaches.

'My eyes really hurt at the end of each day.'

'I spend so much time doing the same process over and over again.'

'My line manager tells me to hurry up all the time. It's really offputting.'

'I am sure my machine must be at least ten years old – the screen flickers and it is difficult to read.'

'I reckon I am going to get this RSI thing, the way I feel at the end of each day.'

'I think I should take it up with the union rep.'

the problem

Explain, with reference to what Trish has said and what you can see in the picture:

(a) to what extent her employer has failed to protect her against VDU hazards

(b) to what extent Trish is herself responsible for her symptoms

How would you advise her to deal with the problem? Write down your advice in the form of bullet points.

5 Accidents and emergencies

this chapter covers . . .

In the last chapter we concentrated on the common types of health, safety and security hazards in the workplace. We examined the ways in which they were dealt with by employees and employers. In this chapter we explain the need to set up procedures for dealing with the more extreme types of hazard:

- accidents and illnesses
- fires
- evacuating the premises for incidents such as fires and bomb alerts
- breaches of security

We also study examples of some of the paperwork that needs to be completed to report incidents of this type.

NVQ PERFORMANCE CRITERIA COVERED

unit 22: CONTRIBUTE TO THE MAINTENANCE OF A HEALTHY, SAFE AND PRODUCTIVE WORKING ENVIRONMENT

element 22.1
Monitor and maintain a safe, healthy and secure working environment

E   follow your organisation's emergency procedures promptly, calmly and efficiently

G   complete any health and safety records legibly and accurately

KNOWLEDGE AND UNDERSTANDING COVERAGE

9   your organisation's emergency procedures

10   how to follow your organisation's emergency procedures and your responsibilities in relation to these

12   health and safety records you may have to complete and how to do so

HELP!

When accidents and emergencies such as fires, bomb threats and injuries occur, whether in the workplace or outside, you should know how to react and what to do. In the workplace there will be established procedures and routines that you will have to learn about and to follow.

what the law requires

The law requires that every employer must:

- communicate emergency and evacuation procedures to employees and other people on the premises
- report major accidents, dangerous occurrences and diseases in the workplace

As we have seen in Chapter 3 of this book, any organisation with five or more employees must have a written **Health and Safety Policy Statement**. This document will normally include details such as:

- the names of people responsible for health and safety, for example the **Safety Officer** and the **First Aider**(s)
- where to find the First Aid box
- where to find the **Accident Book**
- **emergency procedures** – for example how to evacuate the building
- which fire extinguishers to use for different types of fire
- guidance on the handling of dangerous substances
- guidance on manual handling (lifting and moving items in the workplace)

These details should be well known by all employees in a well-run organisation.

We will now examine in a series of Case Studies the way in which employers and employees deal with more serious threats to health and safety in the workplace.

Case Study

THE GUILLOTINE ACCIDENT

Alex has recently started working for an insurance broker and was cutting up some A4 sheets. 'I should use the guillotine if I were you,' said Maria, 'you'll get a much cleaner cut.'

Alex was talking to Maria while he was slicing the paper and unfortunately cut into the fingers of his left hand. He was bleeding profusely and crying out in pain. What should Maria do?

STAY CALM. (run)
ASK TO RAISE ARM. ETC
THEN RUN! TO GET THE 1ST AIDER.

solution

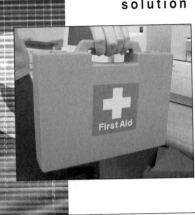

1　Maria stays calm and does not panic.

2　Maria asks around for a First Aider – fortunately her colleague Gail has recently done a British Red Cross First Aid course and is a nominated First Aider for the office. She also saw the accident.

3　Gail fetches the First Aid box.

4　Gail takes charge of the situation, runs Alex's fingers under cold water, sits him down, makes him comfortable, cleans his cuts and bandages the hand. 'He won't need to go to Casualty,' she says, 'but we will need to tell his line manager and make an entry in the Accident Book.'

Accident Report

Full name of injured person　__Alex Branfield__

Job Title　__Admin assistant__　　Department　__Claims__

Date of accident　__12 December 2003__　　Time　__10.40__

Location　__General office__

Details of accident
Cut fingers while operating guillotine. No guillotine guard apparently in place.

Injury sustained
Minor cuts and abrasions to four fingers of left hand.

Witnesses

Name	Job title	Department
Maria Anthony	Admin assistant	Claims
Gail Potter	Senior assistant	Claims

Action Taken
Hand cleaned up and bandaged to staunch bleeding. No need for hospital referral.

Further action necessary
Wound to be monitored and redressed by Gail Potter. Guillotine guard to be checked.

Reported by **Gail Potter**　　Reported to　__Asaf Patel, Line Manager__

Signature　_G M Potter_　　Date　__12 December 2003__

THE IMPORTANCE OF DOCUMENTATION

It is important to complete an Accident Report Form because the document sets out clearly what has happened and who may be responsible.

If the employer is responsible and the employee suffers in the long term as a result, the employee may sue the employer. Suppose Alex is working only part-time and his main occupation is a keyboard player in a band. If his hand is damaged in the long term and he cannot play any more, he may sue for loss of earnings. This is an extreme example, but incidents like this do occur. If a member of the public is injured on the employer's premises, similar legal action could be taken. It is for this reason that it is important that the employer takes out insurance for:

- employee liability – to cover against claims from employees
- public liability – to cover against claims from members of the public

If it is the employee who is at fault, this will be implied in the Accident Report Form and the employer will be better protected against claims from the employee. This is illustrated graphically in the Case Study which follows on the next page.

RIDDOR REPORTING

We have already mentioned RIDDOR (Reporting of Injuries, Diseases and Dangerous Occurrences Regulations 1995) in Chapter 3 (page 49).

These regulations require that the Health and Safety Executive must be notified on official RIDDOR forms of fatal or serious injuries, dangerous occurrences or serious diseases in the workplace. Specifically these regulations require reporting of:

- **death or major injury** in the workplace suffered by an employee, a self-employed person working on the premises or a member of the public; major injuries include – major fractures, amputations, dislocations, loss of sight, burns, electrocution, chemical poisoning (Form F2508)
- **'over three day' injuries** – these are less serious injuries which result in the person injured being off work for three days or more (Form F2508)
- **reportable work-related diseases** – including RSI, skin diseases (from handling dangerous substances), lung diseases (eg asbestosis) and infections such as anthrax and legionnaire's disease (Form F2508A)
- **dangerous occurrences which *could* have resulted in injury** – for example explosions at work, collapse of equipment, escape of radiation, scaffolding collapse, vehicle collisions (Form F2508)

NICO'S ACCIDENT

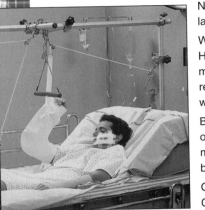

Nico Gambini is employed in the Despatch Department of a large mail order company, Mail2U.

When he was first recruited six months ago, Nico was shown the Health and Safety Policy Statement and made to read the manual handling guidance notes. These made specific reference to the ways in which boxes should be lifted and a warning that not too many boxes should be lifted at one time.

But Nico is a keep-fit and body building fanatic and likes to show off his strength, particularly if the office girls are around. His line manager has told him a number of times not to carry piles of boxes which obscure his vision.

On 19 December, just before the company was closing down for Christmas, Nico was carrying a pile of heavy boxes which were obscuring his forward vision. There was a small step down in the loading bay which was provided with warning signs 'Mind the Step!'. Nico ignored these signs, missed his footing on the step and stumbled forward, dropping the boxes and falling awkwardly on his right arm.

The First Aider was called and it was soon apparent that an ambulance would have to be called: Nico could not move his right arm and was in considerable pain.

Nico was admitted to hospital and was found to have a fracture in his right arm, bruising to his left arm and bruising to his face. The orthopaedic consultant said that it was likely that he would be spending Christmas in a hospital bed.

the paperwork

An Accident Report Form will be completed by Nico's employer. This form is likely to state that a contributory cause of the accident was Nico's disregard for the manual handling guidance notes.

The form will also recommend that:

- the employees working in the Despatch Department are reminded of the manual handling guidance notes
- the employer ensures that the warning notice for the step is seen by despatch department employees

The employer will also have to comply with RIDDOR (Reporting of Injuries, Diseases and Dangerous Occurrences Regulations). These require that the employer must:

- telephone the local Health and Safety Authority (the local authority in this case) immediately and tell them about the business, the injured person and the accident
- within ten days of the accident complete and send to the local authority a completed Form F2508

This form is illustrated on the next two pages.

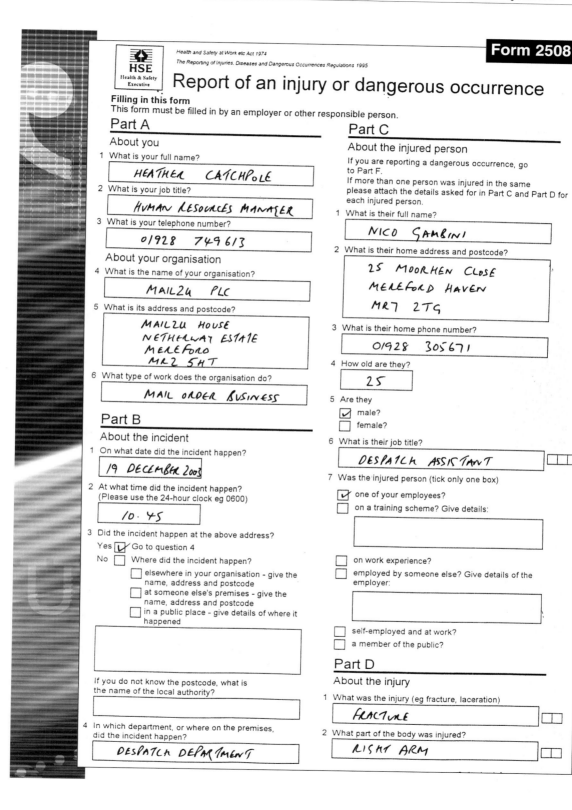

Form 2508

Health and Safety at Work etc Act 1974
The Reporting of Injuries, Diseases and Dangerous Occurrences Regulations 1995

HSE
Health & Safety
Executive

Report of an injury or dangerous occurrence

Filling in this form
This form must be filled in by an employer or other responsible person.

Part A

About you

1 What is your full name?

> HEATHER CATCHPOLE

2 What is your job title?

> HUMAN RESOURCES MANAGER

3 What is your telephone number?

> 01928 749613

About your organisation

4 What is the name of your organisation?

> MAIL24 PLC

5 What is its address and postcode?

> MAIL24 HOUSE
> NETHERWAY ESTATE
> MEREFORD
> MR2 5HT

6 What type of work does the organisation do?

> MAIL ORDER BUSINESS

Part B

About the incident

1 On what date did the incident happen?

> 19 DECEMBER 2008

2 At what time did the incident happen?
(Please use the 24-hour clock eg 0600)

> 10.45

3 Did the incident happen at the above address?
Yes ☑ Go to question 4
No ☐ Where did the incident happen?
☐ elsewhere in your organisation - give the name, address and postcode
☐ at someone else's premises - give the name, address and postcode
☐ in a public place - give details of where it happened

If you do not know the postcode, what is the name of the local authority?

4 In which department, or where on the premises, did the incident happen?

> DESPATCH DEPARTMENT

Part C

About the injured person

If you are reporting a dangerous occurrence, go to Part F.
If more than one person was injured in the same please attach the details asked for in Part C and Part D for each injured person.

1 What is their full name?

> NICO GAMBINI

2 What is their home address and postcode?

> 25 MOORHEN CLOSE
> MEREFORD HAVEN
> MR7 2TG

3 What is their home phone number?

> 01928 305671

4 How old are they?

> 25

5 Are they
☑ male?
☐ female?

6 What is their job title?

> DESPATCH ASSISTANT

7 Was the injured person (tick only one box)
☑ one of your employees?
☐ on a training scheme? Give details:

☐ on work experience?
☐ employed by someone else? Give details of the employer:

☐ self-employed and at work?
☐ a member of the public?

Part D

About the injury

1 What was the injury (eg fracture, laceration)

> FRACTURE

2 What part of the body was injured?

> RIGHT ARM

3 Was the injury (tick the one box that applies)

- [ ] a fatality?
- [x] a major injury or condition? (see accompanying notes) .
- [ ] an injury to an employee or self-employed which prevented them doing their normal work for more than 3 days?
- [ ] an injury to a member of the public which meant they had to be taken from the scene of the accident to a hospital for treatment

4 Did the injured person (tick all the boxes that apply)

- [ ] become unconscious?
- [ ] need resuscitation?
- [x] remain in hospital for more than 24 hours?
- [ ] none of the above?

Part E

About the kind of accident

Please tick the one box that best describes what happened, then go to Part G.

- [ ] Contact with moving machinery or material being machined
- [ ] Hit by a moving, flying or falling object
- [ ] Hit by a moving vehicle
- [ ] Hit something fixed or stationary

- [x] Injured while handling, lifting or carrying
- [ ] Slipped, tripped or fell on the same level
- [ ] Fell from a height
  How high was the fall?

metres

- [ ] Trapped by something collapsing

- [ ] Drowned or asphyxiated
- [ ] Exposed to, or in contact with, a harmful
- [ ] Exposed to fire
- [ ] Exposed to an explosion

- [ ] Contact with electricity or an electrical discharge
- [ ] Injured by an animal
- [ ] Physically assaulted by a person

- [ ] Another kind of accident (describe it in Part G)

Part F

Dangerous occurrences

Enter the number of the dangerous occurrence you are reporting. (The numbers are given in the Regulations in the notes which accompany this form)

Part G

Describing what happened

Give as much detail as you can. For instance

- ∟ the name of any substance involved
- ∟ the name and type of any machine involved
- ∟ the events that led to the incident
- ∟ the part played by any people

If it was a personal injury, give details of what the person was doing. Describe any action that has since been taken to prevent a similar incident. Use a separate piece of paper if you need to.

> MR GAMBINI, WHO IS AN ASSISTANT IN OUR DESPATCH DEPARTMENT SLIPPED AND FELL DOWN A SMALL STEP (10 CM). HE WAS CARRYING A LARGE PILE OF BOXES, WHICH HE DROPPED. HE FELL TO THE FLOOR AND FRACTURED HIS RIGHT ARM IN ATTEMPTING TO BREAK HIS FALL. THERE WERE WARNING SIGNS ABOUT THE STEP, BUT STAFF HAVE AGAIN BEEN ALERTED TO THE HAZARD.

Part H

Your signature

Signature

Date

22/	12	/ 03

Where to send the form
Please send it to the Enforcing Authority for the place where it happened. If you do not know the Enforcing Authority, send it to the nearest HSE office.

For official use		
Client number	Location number	Event number

[ ] INV REP [ ] Y [ ] N

REPORTING DISEASE

An employer whose employee contracts a disease as a result of the workplace environment must report the illness to the Health and Safety Authorities on Form F2508A 'Report of a case of disease.'

Employers are normally advised of serious employee illnesses by the employee's doctor. A typical disease developed by office workers is RSI (Repetitive Strain Injury) caused by overlong periods spent inputting data.

This situation is obviously bad news for the employer because it suggests that Health and Safety regulations are being ignored in the workplace, which could trigger a Health and Safety inspection. Also the employee may be demanding compensation for loss of earnings.

Form F2508A is similar to Form F2508, requiring details of the employer, the employee and the nature of the problem – in this case the circumstances that led to the disease. Extracts from the form are illustrated below.

Part C

The disease you are reporting

1 Please give:

  • the name of the disease, and the type of
    work it is associated with; or

  • the name and number of the disease
    (from Schedule 3 of the Regulations – see
    the accompanying notes).

    LEGIONELLOSIS (19)

2 What is the date of the statement of the doctor who first diagnosed or confirmed the disease?

    23 / 10 / 03

3 What is the name and address of the doctor?

    DR NICHOLAS SPOCK
    HARVEY HOUSE SURGERY
    BROCKWAY ROAD
    MEREFORD
    MR2 2LJ

Part D

Describing the work that led to the disease

Please describe any work done by the affected person which might have led to them getting the disease.

If the disease is thought to have been caused by exposure to an agent at work (eg a specific chemical) please say what that agent is.

Give any other information which is relevant.

Give your description here

    MR NEWTON WAS EMPLOYED
    BY ARCO LIMITED AS MAINTENANCE
    ENGINEER. HE IS THOUGHT TO
    HAVE CONTRACTED THE DISEASE
    WHILE CHECKING THE WATER
    COOLING SYSTEM WHICH WAS
    CONTAMINATED

DEALING WITH FIRES

A fire can be one of the most frightening hazards in the workplace. It can easily be started and it can easily become fatal. Fires can be started by:

- faulty electrical appliances and wiring
- people smoking
- overheating of flammable substances, eg aerosols

Anyone at work – and in the home – has a duty to take care and prevent the incidence of fire.

fire precautions and the law

The UK law relating to fire precautions in the workplace is set out in the Fire Precautions Act 1971 and the Fire Precautions (Workplace) Regulations 1997 (amended 1999), based on European legislation. The law requires that employers should:

- carry out a risk assessment
- provide an adequate number of fire extinguishers and other fire fighting equipment such as fire blankets
- install smoke detectors and fire alarms where appropriate
- train the workforce in dealing with fires – eg with the right type of fire extinguisher
- establish and communicate evacuation procedures to the workforce and also to the public where appropriate
- provide well signed escape routes and exits to a place of safety
- arrange for fire fighting equipment to be regularly checked and maintained

employee familiarity with fire equipment

As noted above, it is the duty of every employer to make sure that employees become familiar with:

- fire fighting equipment in the workplace
- the procedures for evacuating the building in the event of a fire or any other emergency such as bomb scare

Fire extinguishers are the traditional and most effective means of combating fires. But it must be the right form of fire extinguisher, or the fire could be actively encouraged or sensitive equipment could be irretrievably damaged.

The illustrations on the next page show the different types of fire extinguisher. The notes explain what types of fire they should be used for.

which fire extinguisher should I use?

water fire extinguisher

yes for paper, wood, textiles

no for flammable liquids and live electrical equipment

carbon dioxide fire extinguisher

yes for flammable liquids and live electrical equipment

no for paper, wood, textiles

powder fire extinguisher

yes for flammable liquids, gaseous fires, live electrical equipment, paper, wood and textiles

but it will ruin any computer equipment

EVACUATION PROCEDURES

If there is a fire or any other emergency such as a telephoned bomb warning an organisation must have an established **evacuation procedure**. The aim of this procedure is to ensure that all people on the premises can move swiftly and safely out to a nominated place of safety. The evacuation procedure must be communicated to:

- **employees**, by means of regular evacuation drills (normally known as fire drills) and explanation in the Health and Safety Policy Statement and on notices on the premises

- any **members of the public** on the premises – for example in a shop, or in a gym – by prominent signs and notices

FIRE ACTION!

If you discover a fire

1 Sound the alarm.
2 Deal with the fire as far as is safely possible using the equipment provided.
3 Telephone the Fire Services.

If you hear the fire alarm

1 Leave the building by the nearest exit.
2 Report to the assembly point at

the King Street car park

Do not!

1 Take unnecessary risks.
2 Return to the building until authorised to do so.

an evacuation notice

help from the fire services

The Fire Services have a role to play in minimising the risk of fire in the workplace.

They can advise organisations on planning exit routes, placing signs, installing fire exits and fire doors. They can also help with training employees to become the nominated in-house Fire Officers. Note that organisations with twenty or more employees (or eleven or more on an upper floor) require a Fire Certificate, which is awarded after a thorough inspection of the premises.

the evacuation procedure at work

Whenever evacuation takes place, either as a practice 'drill', or in response to a real emergency, there are a number of steps that have to be followed.

As you will see from the notice shown above, if you discover a fire you will need to sound the alarm. If you are unable to deal with the fire (a major electrical fire, for example) you should call the Fire Services on 999 (or whatever your emergency number is).

Most employees will first encounter the evacuation procedures when they hear the alarm sounding. The steps in this case are:

1 Leave the building as quickly and calmly as possible (not sprinting and knocking people over!)

2 Use the quickest and safest designated route – follow the Fire Exit direction signs.

3 Assemble in the designated meeting point.

4 Wait for your name to be called.

5 Return to the place where you work only after (and if) you are authorised to do so.

The person calling the 'register' of names is likely to be the organisation's appointed Safety Officer or a senior manager.

EMPLOYEES' RESPONSIBILITIES AND FIRE RISK

Employees have two main areas of responsibility in relation to fire risk:

- helping to prevent fires starting in the first place
- in the event of a fire helping people with special needs or members of the public who are not familiar with the emergency procedures

helping to prevent fires

There are many bad habits employees can get into which can help fires to start. These should be avoided. The basic rules are:

- ensure that combustible rubbish does not pile up, eg in waste bins in areas where there are smokers (if they are allowed), behind the photocopier or any machinery that runs hot
- avoid obstructing fire escape routes, eg dumping pallets or boxes in front of fire exit doors
- ensure that all Fire Exit signs are not obstructed
- ensure that fire extinguishers are readily accessible
- do not prop open Fire Doors (ie fire-resistant doors which automatically swing shut)
- ensure that any highly flammable material is properly stored
- do not smoke, unless in a 'smoking zone'

Managers too have additional responsibilities. They should:

- ensure that staff are properly trained in the emergency procedures
- hold regular evacuation drills
- ensure that machinery is properly maintained – particularly if it can run hot and endanger flammable substances
- arrange to have fire extinguishers regularly checked

helping other people with evacuation procedures

If there is an evacuation drill or a real emergency, it is possible that there will be people on the premises who are not employees or who have special needs.

Members of the public and visitors should be told what is going on and guided out of the premises.

People with special needs – both employees and customers – will need to be given particular care and attention and will have to be helped out. People in this category include individuals in wheelchairs, the partially sighted and people with a hearing disability which prevents them from hearing the alarm.

DEALING WITH BREACHES OF SECURITY

We have already seen in the last chapter that security hazards can take a number of different forms. They can involve threats from other employees:

- the theft of money left lying around
- the leaking of confidential information

They can also involve threats from outside:

- strangers being allowed in and wandering around the office on false pretences – for example, pretending to be a computer engineer
- allowing exterior doors to be left unattended or unlocked – particularly where there is valuable equipment, money or sensitive information in the office

It is an employee's duty to be alert to incidents such as these and to report them to a superior, a line manager, for example. In the extreme case of intruders on the premises, it will be up to the employee to call Security (or whoever acts as the 'heavy brigade' for the organisation) to investigate and, if necessary, to eject the intruder.

Case Study

DEALING WITH DESPERATE DAN

Dan bought a computer a month ago from Compusale, a computer hardware and software company.

He has had a lot of problems with the machine he bought and has complained on a number of occasions.

You work as a customer services assistant for Compusale in a large open plan office.

You are sitting at your terminal one day and you are confronted with Dan, who has managed to get into your office.

'What are you going to do about my machine then?' he asks angrily 'It's about as much use as a biscuit tin!'

What would you do?

solution

Dan is an intruder. He has no right to be in the office. He poses a serious security threat. You should refuse to talk to him. You should report the matter to your line manager and at the same time contact the Security Division of your company who will arrange for him to be escorted off the premises.

Chapter Summary

- It is important for an employee to know what to do in the event of emergencies such as accidents, illnesses, fires and serious security breaches in the workplace.

- The law requires that an organisation with five or more employees must prepare a Health and Safety Policy Statement which will set out details of emergency procedures to be implemented within the organisation.

- Accidents in the workplace should be recorded in an Accident Book. This will often contain forms which record details of any workplace accidents.

- RIDDOR (Reporting of Injuries, Diseases and Dangerous Occurrences Regulations 1995) require that the Health and Safety Executive is informed immediately in the case of fatal or serious workplace injuries, dangerous occurrences and reportable diseases.

- An employer must by law set up procedures for the evacuation of the premises in the case of emergencies such as fire and bomb threats. These procedures must be communicated to the employees.

- Employees must also know what action to take if there is a security breach; this normally involves reporting the matter to a superior and/or contacting the security people (the 'bouncers') in the organisation.

Key Terms

Safety Officer	a representative chosen (by the union or by the employer) to be responsible for the implementation of safety measures
First Aider	an employee who has had First Aid training and who is responsible for the implementation of First Aid in the workplace
Accident Book	the book which records full details of accidents in the workplace
emergency procedures	procedures set down in the Health and Safety Policy Statement of an organisation which regulate, for example, the way an evacuation is carried out
'over three day' injuries	less serious injuries which result in the injured person being off work for three or more days
dangerous occurrence	an occurrence in the workplace which could have resulted in serious injury, and which will need to be investigated

Student Activities

5.1 List five items which you would expect to find in a company's Health and Safety Policy Statement and which are related to workplace accidents and emergency procedures. *WHERE THE ACCIDENT BOOK IS / WHO IS THE H+S REP / WHO IS THE TRAINED 1ST AIDER / WHERE THE EMERGENCY EXITS ARE / WHERE TO MEET IN AN EMERGENCY. / FIRE EXTINGUIERS*

5.2 Read the description of the incident below, and then answer the questions that follow.

> Percy Pratt works as an accounts assistant in the Finance Office. You are his line manager. He has just made a mug of boiling hot coffee and brought it back to his workstation. He places it on top of his computer, but unfortunately it crashes down over the keyboard, scalding his right hand and ruining the keyboard.
>
> Maria Carey, the First Aider, is also an accounts assistant in the same office and she is called over to help Percy, who is in some pain. She takes him to the washroom and runs cold water over his hands to soothe the pain. She dresses his hands and sends him to the rest room to recover.
>
> She reports back to you:
>
> 'Percy will be OK. He has a slight scalding to the back of his right hand, but I have dressed it. He will probably need to go home to recover, but I see no reason why he should not be in work tomorrow, and I have told him that. We will just need to keep an eye on the scald. I hope the computer keyboard will be alright, but I guess it is a write off!'

    (a)   Who is responsible for this accident? *PERCY PRATT (IT IS PONSIBLE)*

    (b)   You call Percy over to talk about what has happened. He says he is unhappy about the safety measures in the office. How would you reply to this? *1ST) HE HAS NOT BEEN RESPONSIBL FOR HIMSELF + THE SAFETY OF OTHERS + HAS NOT LOOKED AFTER OFFICE EQUIPMENT.*

    (c)   He says that he has heard that the accident will have to be reported under RIDDOR. How would you reply to that? *NO PUT IN ACCIDENTS BOOK HIMSELF + ... + THIS IS ... AS A DANGROUS OCCURANCE...*

    (d)   What action would you recommend be taken in the office following this incident? *NO ONE IS TO PUT A CUP ON TOP OF YOUR P.C / A NEW KEY BOARD + CLEARING OF MESS.*

    (e)   Complete the Accident Report Form on the opposite page in the name of Maria Carey. Use your own name for the line manager to whom she has reported the incident, and today's date.

5.3 What are the three main circumstances in which you would complete a RIDDOR Form 2508? Write a short paragraph explaining each of the three circumstances.

5.4 What type of fire extinguisher is best for:

    (a)   a wastepaper bin fire caused by a dropped match?

    (b)   a computer which has caught fire?

    (c)   the engine of a delivery van which is parked just outside your loading bay?

    In each case justify your choice of extinguisher.

5.5 You have been elected Safety Officer at your place of work. One of your managers asks for a summary of what his staff should do in case the fire alarm goes off. Write down a series of numbered points summarising the emergency procedures in the case of a fire alarm. Make up any details you need to, such as the meeting point. Use details taken from evacuation procedures from your own place of work, if you wish.

Accident Report

Full name of injured person _____

Job Title _____ Department _____

Date of accident _____ Time _____

Location _____

Details of accident

Injury sustained

Witnesses
Name   Job title   Department

Action Taken

Further action necessary

Reported by _____ Reported to _____

Signature _____ Date _____

In this chapter we explain the need for an employee to 'manage' his or her work area. This involves:

- *organising your working area so that you and others can work efficiently and also comply with the organisation's rules and requirements for the workplace*

- *identifying and dealing with problems relating to your work area, either sorting them out yourself, or referring them to someone who can*

- *dealing with workplace equipment correctly, by following the manufacturer's instructions and any guidelines set down by your organisation*

NVQ PERFORMANCE CRITERIA COVERED

unit 22   **CONTRIBUTE TO THE MAINTENANCE OF A HEALTHY, SAFE AND PRODUCTIVE WORKING ENVIRONMENT**

element 22.1
Monitor and maintain an effective and efficient working environment

A   *organise the work area you are responsible for, so that you and others can work efficiently*

B   *organise the work area you are responsible for, so that it meets your organisation's requirements and presents a positive image of yourself and your team*

C   *identify conditions around you that interfere with effective working*

D   *put right any conditions that you can deal with safely, competently, within the limits of your authority and with the agreement of other relevant people*

E   *promptly and accurately report any other conditions to the relevant person*

F   *use and maintain equipment in accordance with manufacturer's instructions and your organisation's procedures*

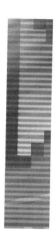

AN 'EFFECTIVE' AND 'EFFICIENT' WORKING ENVIRONMENT?

NVQ Element 22.2 stresses the need for an 'effective' and an 'efficient' working environment.

What exactly do these terms mean?

'Effective' means getting the result that you want. In football an effective defence prevents the opposing team scoring goals, in the dating game an effective chat-up line will win you the partner you have your eye on. An **effective working environment** will result in the achievement of the objectives of the organisation, for example – a motivated workforce, sales and profit targets achieved or exceeded.

'Efficient' is not the same as 'effective'. It means getting the job done with the minimum waste of effort and resources. This is, of course, an important objective in any organisation. But note that an **efficient working environment** will not always be 'effective'. A line manager, for example, may be ruthlessly efficient in saving time and money, but the workforce may be demotivated and levels of performance will fall off. The working environment will become less 'effective'.

The ideal working environment, therefore, is one that **balances effectiveness and efficiency**. The job is done well with the minimum wastage of effort and resources.

In this chapter we will discuss the role of the employee in making sure that the working environment – the immediate work area and the 'office' as a whole – is both effective and efficient. The two key factors in this are:

• being organised

• being aware of the needs of other employees and the organisation

ORGANISING THE WORK AREA

what is the 'work area'?

An employee's work area is not just the desk or workstation, it is the area which surrounds it, involving desk, chair and any furniture and filing cabinets in the vicinity.

The state of the work area is the responsibility of the employee – the user. The way in which it is (or is not) organised says a great deal about the user.

it helps to be organised

A tidy desk normally means a tidy mind, just as an untidy work area often indicates a person who finds organisation rather a struggle.

An organised work area has a number of characteristics:

- it is tidy
- it is clean
- the user knows where everything is and can find it quickly
- everything is within easy reach
- the computer is correctly set up
- the chair is correctly adjusted for the user

The test of a well-organised work area is whether the user's colleagues can also find what they want. Suppose the user is an accounts assistant who deals with sales orders. She is out at lunch and an important customer telephones and asks if a recently issued sales order can be checked as an incorrect catalogue code may have been quoted on the document. Can the sales order be found? Is it in an organised filing system or pending tray, or is it buried under a pile of unsorted papers? Worse still, is it there at all?

It is not difficult to see from this that if a work area is organised properly, it will be:

- **effective** because tasks can be completed and the job done
- **efficient** because time (and therefore money) will not be wasted

the importance of efficiency

Examples of **efficiency** in the working environment are:

- having resources that you need within easy reach and not in a filing cabinet at the other end of the office

- carrying out tasks in the time allotted – other people may be waiting for you to finish checking documents so that they can carry out a task
- not wasting resources such as photocopy paper
- taking care of resources so that they will last, eg storing computer disks correctly

Efficiency is important not only because cutting down on wastage means greater profit for the organisation, but also because it has a direct influence on the **effectiveness** of other members of a workplace team.

THE ORGANISATION'S RULES FOR THE WORK AREA

Just as a teenager covers his or her room walls with 'statement' posters, employees like to personalise their working environment in order to establish their identity in the workplace and provide a psychological sense of security.

personalising the work area

Examples of this include:

- photographs of friends and family
- postcards received at work
- small posters saying things like 'you don't have to be mad to work here, but it helps'
- 'toys' – eg executive puzzles and fluffy animals
- plants
- bowls of fruit

An employee's work area will tell you a lot about that employee.

The organisation will, however, have **guidelines** which will regulate the extent to which an employee can put up posters, postcards and other items. It is unlikely that these guidelines will be written down, but they will normally be based on a test of what is 'reasonable' and be enforced either by a line manager or by the comments of colleagues objecting to what they think is unreasonable!

*a customer services desk
- subject to strict guidelines*

What *is* 'reasonable'? This depends on the nature of the workplace. If it is a closed office which is rarely visited by outsiders, each employee is likely to have the freedom to personalise his or her work area, as long as what is displayed is not offensive to colleagues or to management.

If the office is open plan and open to the public gaze, the organisation is likely to require that personal items should be unobtrusive. A bank customer services desk, for example will be kept very tidy and have welcoming features, such as flowers, as in the illustration on the left. The posters on the wall here are not the employees' personal choice but advertise the products of the organisation.

The working environment in this illustration gives a very positive image to the public of the financial services team that operates in the office.

DEALING WITH WORKING CONDITIONS

We have seen earlier in this book that health and safety laws and regulations set down guidelines for the physical working environment. For example:

1   The workplace should allow at least 3.715m^2 of floor space and at least 11 cubic metres of space to each employee.

2   The temperature of the office should be not less than 16°C after the first hour of work.

3   The office should be effectively ventilated by fresh or purified air.

4   There must be adequate natural or artificial light.

5   The office must be cleaned regularly and frequently, and rubbish cleared away.

6   There should be sufficient toilet and washing facilities.

It is the responsibility of the employee to identify conditions in the working environment that interfere with effective working, for example a workplace that is:

- too cramped or poorly laid out
- too hot or too cold

- too stuffy or too draughty
- too bright or too dim
- too noisy

Problems like this can reduce both the **effectiveness** (getting things done) and the **efficiency** (getting things done with the minimum of wastage) of the workplace. For example:

- an office with poor heating will reduce the ability of the employees to work: some tasks may not get done and other tasks will take much longer, costing the organisation more
- poor air quality may result in staff illness: again some tasks may not get done and the organisation is likely to have the extra cost of sick pay

Sometimes the employee can do something about problems like these, and should take action. Sometimes the employee will have to refer the problem to someone else. This is illustrated in the Case Study which follows.

Case Study

GETTING IT SORTED

Jo is an accounts assistant at Spira PLC, an insurance company, based in Staines.

When she started work in the office she got on well with her colleagues, but she noticed that the working environment was not as ideal as her previous office at Sanitas Limited where she trained in accounts work.

situation

Jo has noted a number of problems and wonders how she should deal with them. Should she take action herself or should she refer them to Rashid Singh, the Line Manager? The problems are as follows:

1   Jo's desk is awkwardly situated by the photocopier. She is disturbed by people using the machine, and doesn't like the fumes it gives off. She notices that there is a space for a desk nearer to the workstations which deal with the sales and purchases processing.

2   The office is very warm to work in, particularly in the afternoon when the computers have been running for a while. The heating comes from an air conditioning system which has a thermostatic switch on the office wall. Jo often feels very sleepy after lunch and sometimes goes home with a headache. She talks to her colleagues about this and they agree with her – the office needs to be cooler and fresher, and then they will all work better.

3   The office has a big window through which the sun shines for much of the day. There are blinds, but they are stuck in the open position, and Jo, along with many of the staff, finds the light so dazzling that she cannot see her computer screen properly.

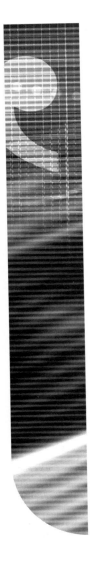

solutions:

problem 1 – the desk

Jo's desk is awkwardly situated by the photocopier. She works inefficiently because she is some distance from the accounts workstations. Her position also affects her effectiveness because of the fumes from the machine. She obviously cannot drag the desk across the office, and office layout is not a matter about which she can make decisions. So she will have to refer the problem to Rashid, her line manager. If there is space in the part of the office she has identified, Rashid can arrange to have the desk moved, but not before careful measurements have been made and the matter referred to the office staff.

problem 2 – feeling the heat

Temperature and air quality in an office are critical factors for effective working. If the working environment is too hot, as could be the case here, people become drowsy and headachy; if the office is too cold, people are uncomfortable and distracted from their work. A further aspect of the problem is that some people like higher temperatures than others. The situation in this office, as in many other offices, is that the temperature rises in the afternoon. The solution is for Jo to discuss the matter with her colleagues, in one of their regular team meetings, for example. If there is a majority in favour of turning the heating down – which can easily be done using the thermostatic control on the wall – Jo could do this at the appropriate time of day. She would, of course, have to consult first with Rashid, her line manager, but he is unlikely to object.

problem 3 – the stuck blinds

Dazzling sunshine can be very pleasant on a beach, but can reduce effectiveness and efficiency in a workplace. Jo and her colleagues find that not being able to see a VDU properly results in eyestrain. The solution here is simple. Jo shows some initiative and one lunchtime spends half-an-hour untangling the cords which operate the blinds. They can now be opened and closed normally, to the benefit of everyone. This is not a problem which Jo needs to refer to a line manager or even to all her colleagues – she just takes a decision and gets on with it.

USING AND MAINTAINING EQUIPMENT

The working environment – particularly the office – normally has a wide variety of complex and delicate equipment which is in daily use. For example, an accounts assistant may have to use:

- computer hardware – processing units, backup devices, printers
- fax machine
- photocopier
- credit card terminal
- shredder

We have seen earlier in this book that both the employer and the employee have duties of care under Health and Safety regulations when using this type of equipment. In this chapter we look at the guidance that exists for the operation and maintenance of equipment in the workplace. This guidance can be found in:

- the instructions provided with the equipment – this may take the form of a manual, a sheet, or online assistance

- separate guidelines issued by the employer

The important point here is that these guidelines and instructions must be followed:

- when setting the equipment up and while operating the equipment

- when something goes wrong

- when maintenance is needed

always read the instructions!

An employee should never adopt his or her own remedy.

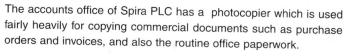

Case Study

DEALING WITH THE PHOTOCOPIER

The accounts office of Spira PLC has a photocopier which is used fairly heavily for copying commercial documents such as purchase orders and invoices, and also the routine office paperwork.

The photocopier was bought outright by the business a couple of years ago, and there is a maintenance contract with Photoserve Limited, which provides toner, annual maintenance and a call out service in case of major breakdowns.

In the office there is a printed sheet of internal regulations governing the use of the photocopier by employees. This is shown below.

PHOTOCOPIER USE

1 No unauthorised copying.
2 No copying of copyright material (with © symbol) without reference to line manager.
3 Switch copier off at the end of the day, but leave on at mains.
4 Renew paper in cassette tray if 'paper out' light is on.
5 Toner to be replaced by senior assistants only.
6 If you cannot clear a paper jam, please refer to senior assistant.
7 Refer major faults to line manager.
8 If the maintenance light or call light is on, refer to line manager.

The manufacturer's instructions for the photocopier are set out in a booklet, but this is rarely used because most of the common instructions are printed on the top panel of the photocopier. Some of these are illustrated below and to the right.

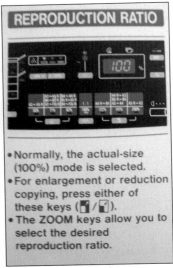

REPRODUCTION RATIO

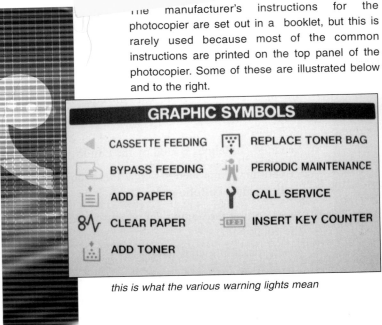

GRAPHIC SYMBOLS

◀	CASSETTE FEEDING	▥	REPLACE TONER BAG
	BYPASS FEEDING		PERIODIC MAINTENANCE
	ADD PAPER	⚚	CALL SERVICE
8∿	CLEAR PAPER		INSERT KEY COUNTER
	ADD TONER		

this is what the various warning lights mean

- Normally, the actual-size (100%) mode is selected.
- For enlargement or reduction copying, press either of these keys (▥ / ▥).
- The ZOOM keys allow you to select the desired reproduction ratio.

this tells you how to reduce or to enlarge copies

The staff of Spira PLC therefore have to know about the company procedures for dealing with the photocopier and also the operating instructions on the machine itself. Some of these relate to each other, as you will see if you carry out Student Activity 6.5 on page 92.

Chapter Summary

- It is important that an employee organises his or her work area so that work can be carried out efficiently and effectively by all employees who use that work area.

- Employees naturally like to bring personal items into the workplace. When doing so, they should take notice of the organisation's guidelines and also their colleagues' views on what is acceptable. The aim should be to give a positive image both to colleagues and to outsiders who are visiting.

- Employees should be able to identify problems with the working environment – such as noise, heat and lighting conditions – which might interfere with effective and efficient working. They should be able to decide whether to deal with the problems themselves, in consultation with colleagues, or whether to refer them to an appropriate person.

- Equipment in the work area will normally be provided with the manufacturer's instructions for the use and maintenance of that equipment. The organisation may also provide written guidelines for the use of the equipment. It is the responsibility of every employee to be aware of the instructions and guidelines and to take notice of them when using the equipment and encountering problems.

Key Terms		
work area	the desk and chair at which an employee works, plus the area and furniture which surrounds it
effective work area	a work area which enables tasks to be completed and targets met
efficient work area	a work area in which resources are not wasted
work area guidelines	the organisation's policy for allowing personal items into the work area – it will vary according to how public the working area is
work area conditions	the physical aspects – heat, air, noise, light – of the working environment which affect employees' performance
use and maintenance	the operation of workplace equipment (use) and the need to keep the equipment in good working order (maintenance)

Student Activities

Note

It is appreciated that not all students will be in employment. The questions that follow ask you to comment on workplace situations. If you are not in employment you should try to put yourself in the place of someone who is. If you are unsure about this, you could ask friends who have jobs, or you could even watch TV programmes which feature office life.

6.1 Explain the difference between an 'effective' working environment and an 'efficient' working environment.

6.2 (a) Write down three characteristics of a well-organised work area.

(b) Describe three annoying incidents (real or imaginary) which would result from a poorly-organised work area.

How would the incidents in (b) affect the effectiveness and efficiency of the working environment?

6.3 Make a list of personal items which you would <u>like</u> to have in your own work space (real or imaginary). Do you think you are likely to be allowed these items:

(a) in an office which is normally closed to the public and has few visitors?

(b) in an open-plan office which has a reception desk for the public (eg bank, insurance office, estate agent)?

Explain – with reasons – why some of your chosen items may be objected to, and who would object to them in (a) and in (b).

6.4   How would you deal with the following situations which relate to conditions in the working environment which are affecting your rate of work? Would you take the decision yourself? Consult with your colleagues? Refer the matter to your line manager?

(a)   The office is too hot, and you have an electric fan at home. You want to bring it in to put on your desk.

(b)   The office is too cold in the mornings – the office thermometer reads 15°C. You have an oil heater at home which you would like to bring in to put under your desk to warm you up.

(c)   The office is too stuffy in summer, but if you open the window everybody hears the noise from the building site on the other side of the road.

(d)   The fluorescent light above your desk is flickering and really annoying you.

6.5   Read the photocopier Case Study on pages 89 and 90 and explain what action you would take in the circumstances listed below. Refer in each case to the internal notice 'Photocopier Use' and to the illustrations of the manufacturer's instructions on the top of the photocopier.

(a)   The photocopier runs out of paper.

(b)   The photocopier paper jams and the jam light 8⚡ comes on.

(c)   The toner out light ⊡ comes on.

(d)   A colleague asks you to photocopy a funny cartoon from today's newspaper.

(e)   Your line manager asks you to photocopy some of the stock market share prices from today's newspaper.

(f)   A colleague asks you to photocopy a couple of chapters from a training manual which the office has bought. You notice that '© Enigma Training 2003' is printed on the front cover.

(g)   Your line manager asks you to photocopy a couple of internally-produced reports. They contain some charts which are 150% larger than the normal page size you are copying.

(h)   You are photocopying some invoices and the display panel suddenly starts flashing a light, which shows a symbol which looks like a maintenance engineer.

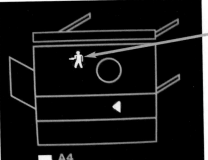

Unit 23

Achieving personal effectiveness

what this unit is about

This unit is concerned with the personal and organisational aspects of an employee's role. In the first element you need to show that you can plan and organise your work effectively and demonstrate that you prioritise your activities. The second element requires you to demonstrate that you work effectively with others by offering assistance, resolving difficulties, and meeting deadlines. In the final element in this unit you need to show that you develop yourself through learning and acquiring new skills and knowledge.

The Unit is dealt with by three chapters, each covering one of the elements:

Element 23.1	Chapter 7	**Plan and organise your work**
Element 23.2	Chapter 8	**Working with others**
Element 23.3	Chapter 9	**Improving your performance**

7 Plan and organise your work

In this chapter we explain the need for an employee to plan and organise his or her work so that the objectives of the organisation can be met and the work carried out efficiently. This involves a number of processes:

- identifying the various tasks that have to be carried out in the workplace

- organising them in order of priority so that the requirements of the organisation and its other employees can be met

- using planning aids such as diaries and schedules to organise tasks

- identifying when priorities change and knowing how to modify schedules

- asking for help and advice when priorities do change

- letting the right person know when problems are encountered in getting the work done

- organising tasks so that the requirements of the law and other regulations can be met

NVQ PERFORMANCE CRITERIA COVERED

unit 23   ACHIEVING PERSONAL EFFECTIVENESS

element 23.1

Plan and organise your own work

A   identify and prioritise tasks according to organisational procedures and regulatory requirements

B   recognise changes in priorities and adapt resources allocations and work plans accordingly

C   use appropriate planning aids to plan and monitor work progress

D   identify, negotiate and co-ordinate relevant assistance to meet specific demands and deadlines

E   report anticipated difficulties in meeting deadlines to the appropriate person

F   check that work methods and activities conform to legal and regulatory requirements and organisational procedures

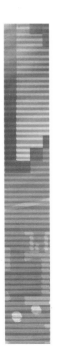

KNOWLEDGE AND UNDERSTANDING COVERAGE

1   *Relevant legislation: copyright, data protection, equal opportunities*

2   *Sources of legal requirements: Data Protection, Companies Acts*

4   *Employee responsibilities in complying with the relevant legislation*

5   *Work methods and practices in your organisation*

6   *Handling confidential information*

14   *The scope and limit of your own authority for taking corrective actions*

16   *Target setting, prioritising and organising work*

17   *Work planning and scheduling techniques and aids*

18   *Time management*

23   *Deadlines and timescales*

24   *Dealing with changed priorities and unforeseen situations*

26   *Negotiating the assistance of others*

27   *Co-ordinating resources and tasks*

28   *The organisational and department structure*

29   *Own work role and responsibilities*

31   *Reporting procedures*

WORKING IN AN ORGANISATION

why work?

Employees normally come to work, not just to earn money (although many claim this as their sole motive!) but because the workplace, like a family, is a social grouping of people who work, argue and have a laugh together. By going to work, employees gain a unique sense of identity which the organisation and social grouping provides. The idea of the workplace as an extended 'family' or 'team' was vigorously promoted by the Japanese and adopted by Western business culture. Its origin, of course, has deeper roots. The chocolate manufacturer, Cadburys, which promoted the ethic of hard work and benefits for all, built a whole 'village' to house its employees – its 'extended family' – over fifty years ago.

The reason for making this point is that employees learn to treat the workplace as an environment in which they have a sense of 'social' responsibility for what they do. This responsibility extends to:

- the everyday tasks that they have to carry out

- their attitude to their colleagues when they carry out tasks

- the idea that they are working together to achieve common **objectives** adopted by the organisation

employees and objectives

What are these 'objectives' of an organisation? They may well include:

- customer satisfaction – making the customer the main focus of the organisation
- profitability – which should benefit employees, owners and customers
- sustainability – reducing wastage of natural resources, eg energy and paper

In order to achieve these objectives, organisations promote:

- customer care schemes
- profit-sharing schemes
- 'green' schemes to cut down on wastage, eg of energy and paper

These objectives can affect the way employees are required to carry out their day-to-day tasks. The example below shows how a Customer Care scheme in a major financial services organisation sets very specific targets for the performance of workplace tasks. Therefore, when an assistant sorts out a customer query, it is not just a case of 'that's another one out of the way' but 'I got a buzz of satisfaction in showing that our organisation cares about its customers.' In short, tasks are often seen to be related to objectives.

---

day-to-day tasks in a Customer Care scheme

efficiency

- aim to be 100% error free
- answer all letters within 2 days of receipt
- advise customers of delivery timescales

problem solving

- take ownership – don't blame others
- resolve complaints within 2 to 10 working days
- follow up afterwards to ensure that the customer is satisfied

courtesy

- greet customers and smile
- use customer's name
- give customer 100% of your attention

dealing with customers who are waiting

- serve all customers within 4 minutes
- apologise if a customer is kept waiting
- make visible efforts to reduce waiting times

using the telephone

- answer before the third ring, if possible
- speak clearly to customers, use their name and check their understanding of what you say

organisational procedures

The way in which employees tackle tasks is often set down in written sets of **procedures**. Larger organisations are likely to have manuals which give guidance; smaller organisations may have written 'checklists' compiled by experienced staff. Examples of jobs in an accounting context which will have set procedures for the tasks carried out include:

- supermarket cashiers dealing with cash, debit and credit cards
- employees processing payroll
- accounts assistants paying customer invoices

The example shown below is a set of procedures for a shop taking payment by debit and credit card.

---

procedures for taking payment by debit and credit card

■ Swipe the card through the card reader.

■ The terminal checks automatically that

- the card number is valid
- the card has not been lost or stolen
- there are sufficient funds to pay for the transaction

■ If the terminal refuses the transaction, request the customer to pay using another way, eg cash.

■ If the amount is above the floor limit, a telephone call to the card merchant will be required to authorise the transaction.

■ The till prints a two-part receipt which includes space for the cardholder's signature.

■ The customer signs the customer copy, and the signature is compared with that on the card.

■ Hand the top copy of the receipt to the customer. The signed copy must be stored in the till and filed away at the end of the shift in case of a future query.

'what next?'

So far in this chapter we have seen that an employee normally has sets of instructions and procedures to learn when doing a job. These are laid down by the organisation. The employee is also made to appreciate that as a member of a team, he or she is helping the organisation achieve its objectives, customer care being a common example.

The focus of this Unit is on planning and organisation. The day-to-day work will involve a wide variety of tasks competing for the employee's time. The question 'what next?' involves identifying and prioritising the tasks that need to be done. We will now examine the techniques and aids available to the employee.

WHAT ARE MY TASKS?

keeping to the job description

An employee needs to know:

- what tasks need to be done in the office
- what tasks the employee is able to do in the office

These are not necessarily the same. Employees should be given a **job description** which sets out exactly what the employee is expected to be able to do. It may be that a line manager puts pressure onto an employee to carry out tasks which the employee is not qualified or able to do. The employee may think 'promotion here we come!' but also may get in a mess and make mistakes for which he or she should not really be held responsible.

One golden rule is therefore to look at your job description and know what you should have to do and what limits there are to your range of activities.

identifying types of tasks

The next golden rule is to be able to identify exactly what tasks have to be done and to identify what type of tasks they are, because this will affect the order in which you will carry them out.

There are a number of different types of task, for example, in an accounts office . . .

- **routine tasks**

  These are everyday tasks such as reading the post and emails, checking invoices, inputting runs of data, sending standard letters, answering telephone queries, photocopying and filing. They do not hold any great surprises, but their efficient completion is important to the smooth running of the office.

- **non-routine tasks**

  These are the unexpected tasks such as helping with one-off projects, working out of the office on a special assignment, or helping to clear up after the washroom has flooded. These may hold up your normal routine work.

Routine tasks are easy to plan for because they are predictable.

Non-routine tasks cannot be planned for, and they can sometimes cause problems, as we will see later in the chapter. They call for flexibility and logical thinking, skills which to some extent can be developed.

As you will know some people thrive on routine and do not like it to be upset; others get bored by it and enjoy the challenges of the unexpected.

In addition, tasks may be **urgent** and they may be **important**. These are not always the same thing . . .

- **urgent tasks**

  These are tasks which have to be done by a specific pressing deadline: the MD may need a spreadsheet immediately for a meeting currently taking place; customer statements may have to go out in tonight's post.

- **important tasks**

  These are tasks for which you have been given personal responsibility. They may be part of your normal routine and other people depend on their successful completion, or they may have been delegated to you because your line manager thinks you capable of them.

working out the priorities

Prioritising tasks means deciding on which order the tasks should be carried out. Which one first? Which one last? Which tasks matter? Which tasks do not matter so much?

The guide to the basic order of priority is shown below. You may, of course, think of exceptions to this rule, particularly with items 2 and 3.

an order of priority . . .

1
Tasks that are **urgent and important** – they have got to be done soon and if you do not do them you are going to let a lot of people down – eg producing the spreadsheet for the MD's meeting.

2
Tasks that are **urgent but less important**, eg watering office plants which have dried out – if you fail to water them straightaway the job still needs doing, but the office is not going to grind to a halt if they remain dry.

3
Tasks that are **important but not urgent**, eg producing some sales figures for your line manager for a meeting at the end of the week – the task has to be done, but it could be done tomorrow.

4
Tasks that are **neither important nor urgent**, eg archiving material from some old files. This task is a useful 'filler' when the office becomes less busy; it would not matter, however, if it were put off for a week or two.

FLICK'S DAY – WORKING OUT THE PRIORITIES

Flick works as an accounts assistant at the Liverpool head office of Estro PLC, a company that makes vacuum cleaners. Her main job is to process the incoming sales orders. She is supervised by her line manager Josie Khan.

She is not having a good week and seems stressed by the workload she has been given. It is Thursday 6 February and things are getting no better.

She has written down her tasks on various bits of paper and has stuck post-it notes on the side of her computer screen, marking them 'Remember!' Her colleague, Kirsty, has written notes to her. She also has her daily routine sheet which came with her job description.

These are all shown below.

SALES ORDER PROCESSING: DAILY ROUTINE

1 Collect mail, open, sort and refer where necessary
2 Open email and deal with queries - refer where necessary
3 Check incoming sales orders and debit notes
4 Check sales orders with credit control lists
5 Batch and process sales orders on computer
6 Print sales invoices and credit notes
7 Check printed documents
8 Agree batch total with computer day book summary
9 Pass invoices and credit notes for checking against order documentation
10 File copy invoices, credit notes and order documentation
11 Answer customer queries - refer where necessary

These are the notes received from Kirsty, a colleague:

Flick - Accounts Manager wants January sales figures asap!

Kirsty 6 Feb 9.30

Flick - we are moving the computers at 2.00 Thursday afternoon - can you help? Kirsty

These are the 'Remember!' post-it notes Flick has stuck on the side of her computer screen:

> **REMEMBER!**
> Get instant coffee for staff kitchen. Ordinary <u>and</u> decaff! Both jars now empty.

> **REMEMBER!**
> **4 FEB**
> Josie wants printouts of top 10 customer activity reports by end of Friday.

> **REMEMBER!**
> Old customer sales files need moving to separate filing drawer some time.

How is Flick going to work out her priorities?

solution

Flick takes a short morning break to discuss her various tasks with her line manager, Josie. At Josie's suggestion she thinks about the priorities involved and classifies the tasks according to how urgent they are and how important they are. She starts by prioritising the non-routine/unexpected tasks:

urgent and important tasks

- The Accounts Manager wants the January sales figures straightaway.
- The computers have to be moved at 2.00 pm that day.

urgent and less important tasks

- The staff kitchen needs more coffee.

important and non-urgent tasks

- The top 10 customer activity reports are required for Friday.

less important and non-urgent tasks

- The old customer sales files need moving to a separate filing drawer.

The non-routine tasks are fairly easily prioritised, as seen above, although there was some uncertainty over whether the staff coffee or the customer printouts had greater priority! But Flick's problem was how to combine the non-routine tasks with the big pile of routine paperwork she had to get through that day. Then there was the filing to do and customers on the telephone with 'stupid' queries.

Josie, her line manager, suggests that she should deal with her tasks in the following order:

1 urgent and important tasks – the January sales figures, shifting the computers
2 important routine tasks – these include processing and checking documentation, answering customer queries
3 urgent and less important tasks – it will not take long to get some more coffee
4 important and non-urgent tasks – the printouts for the next day (Friday)
5 less important and non-urgent tasks – filing (daily filing and shifting old files)

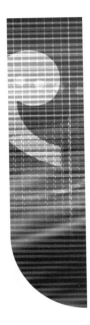

Josie also suggests that Flick compiles a prioritised 'To Do' list of all her non-routine tasks. She can then tick off the items as she does them. This will replace all the notes and Post-it stickers she has all over her desk. It can also be updated as she is asked to carry out new non-routine tasks.

FLICK'S 'TO DO' LIST

1   January sales figures for the Accounts Manager.

2   Thursday 2.00 pm move computers.

3   Coffee - get jars of ordinary and decaff at lunch time.

4   Print out top 10 customer activity reports for Josie, Friday.

5   Move old customer sales files to new drawer, as and when.

USING PLANNING AIDS

The Case Study on the last few pages has shown how an employee has become more effective by becoming more organised and prioritising tasks. The Post-it notes are important in the process, but they are only a start. There are a number of planning aids available to help with organisation, time planning and prioritisation. These include:

- a 'To Do' list – as seen above
- a diary
- a planning schedule
- an action plan

'To Do' lists

Making lists of things 'to do' are very common both at work and at home, ranging from the type of list shown above to the very basic family shopping list. It is the organised person, however, who writes these lists on an ongoing basis, possibly daily, incorporating actions which have not been ticked off on the previous day in a new list. In other words, tasks that have not been done are carried forward onto a new list. Lists may be written on paper or they may be compiled on the computer as a form of electronic 'Post-it' note.

'To do' lists may be subdivided to show the priorities of the tasks to be done. Look at the example below.

'TO DO' LIST   1 April

urgent stuff

1   Aged debtors schedules for the Accounts Manager for today.

2   Sales summaries for Costings section for today.

3   Get March statements in the post today.

non-urgent

1   Print out activity reports for overseas customers.

2   Set up spreadsheet for regional sales analysis.

3   Look into venues for staff evening out.

---

diaries

The diary organises tasks in terms of time. They are very useful planning aids and ensure – if they are efficiently kept – that tasks and events do not clash. Diaries can be paper-based or electronic. They can be individual diaries or office or 'section' diaries used for a group of employees.

The traditional paper-based diary with a week to view can be used alongside 'To do' lists as an efficient way of time planning and prioritising. Some people keep the 'To do' lists in their diary. The diary shown below is kept by a line manager.

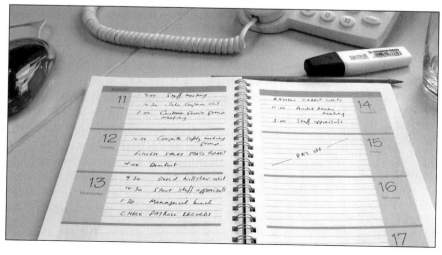

planning schedules

Planning schedules are rather more complex planning devices which deal with situations such as projects where:

- some tasks *have to* follow on from each other – to give a simple example, you have to boil the water before making a cup of coffee – these are known as **critical** activities; you cannot achieve what you want without doing them in sequence

- some tasks are **non-critical** – they are important, but the timing is not so crucial – you will have to put coffee in the cup, but you can do it while the kettle is boiling or even the day before if you want!

So whether you are making coffee or planning a space launch, the principles remain the same. Sometimes there will be a non-routine activity in the workplace, which is complicated and involves a number of inter-dependent tasks. Organisations often use a visual representation of the tasks in the form of horizontal bars set against a time scale to help with the planning. These are known as Gannt charts and can be drawn up manually, or, more often these days, on the computer screen using dedicated software.

It is unlikely that you will have to plan a project in this way, but you may well have to interpret a chart to see *how* you or your section will be involved, and *when*. The Case Study below shows what happens when an office relocates.

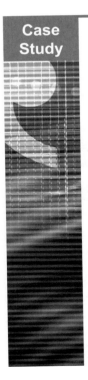

Case Study

HERMES BUREAU: A PLANNING SCHEDULE

situation

You work for a computer bureau – Hermes Bureau – which provides accounting, payroll and other computer services to a wide range of commercial customers.

The business plans to invest in new premises shortly, and has purchased the lease of an office in the town, and will be able to move in six months' time.

The management of Hermes is taking the opportunity when moving to update its computer hardware and software systems.

There are a number of important tasks to carry out before the business moves, and the management has drawn up the list set out on the next page. The software needs updating and customising by programmers, and this will be the task which will take the most time. You see that all the tasks will have to be completed before the new office can become operational, and the obvious fact that the ordering of software and hardware can only take place after full assessment. The management allows itself a clear two week planning period before starting the process.

Hermes is very busy at the moment. When should the planning start?

Task A	time available for detailed planning	2 weeks
Task B	assessment of computer hardware	2 weeks
Task C	ordering new computers	2 weeks
Task D	assessment of new software	4 weeks
Task E	ordering software	10 weeks
Task F	obtaining quotes from removal firm	3 weeks
Task G	ordering the removal van	3 weeks

solution

The Gannt planning chart drawn up by Hermes Bureau shows:

- the activities on a weekly schedule (the weeks are numbered across the top)
- the critical activities as black bars
- the activities which are not critical as grey bars
- float times for non-critical activities – ie times during which a delay can occur which will not hold up the project – as white bars

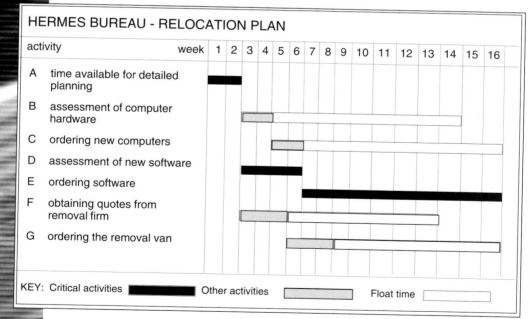

HERMES BUREAU - RELOCATION PLAN

You can also see from this chart that the black bars represent the *priority* activities: planning, software assessment and software ordering. The grey bars are the non-priority activities which can be slotted in when convenient. What you effectively have in this chart is the type of prioritised list seen earlier in this chapter, but a prioritised list set on a time schedule. The visual aspect of the chart makes it easier to understand.

action plans

After a series of activities has been scheduled over time, as in the last Case Study, the organisation can then carry out more detailed planning in the form of an **action plan** which will:

- define each activity in detail
- establish start dates for individual activities
- establish target finish dates
- state who is responsible for carrying out each activity
- in some cases state the cost of each activity

This form of plan is a form of checklist which can be regularly monitored and amended as required. Plans rarely go according 'to plan'. Computer spreadsheets are often used for setting out action plans because they can be easily amended and printed out in revised form.

The example below shows an action plan used in a marketing department which is launching a new product. As the months pass, the plan will be monitored, updated and actual costs checked to see if they are within budget (as you may have seen in your Unit 4 studies).

Enigma Limited

marketing action plan

Product 247G - launch date April

Month	Activity	Person in charge	completed	budget £	actual £
Feb	Book press adverts - trade magazines	RP	6 Feb	5,600	5,750
Feb	Leaflet design	HG	12 Feb	1,200	1,200
Feb	Catalogue design	HG	12 Feb	2,400	2,750
March	Leaflet printing	GF		12,000	
March	Catalogue printing	GF		34,500	
March	Press releases	DD		100	
April	Public launch on 1 April	DD		50,000	
April	Leaflet mailings	DD		5,600	
April	Catalogue mailings	DD		7,500	
April	Mailing of samples	VF		3,500	
May	Telesales to follow mailings	DD		2,400	

MONITORING AND CHANGING PRIORITIES

So far in this chapter we have dealt with the techniques for planning and prioritising tasks. We have also looked at the planning aids that can be used, ranging from simple 'To Do' checklists to complex schedules and action plans for projects.

the importance of monitoring

But things never go quite according to plan. The unexpected can occur and what seems like a quiet productive day can turn into a stressful time, full of awkward decisions. An important aspect of working is therefore **monitoring** what is going on. Is everything going to plan? If it is, tasks can be carried out in the decided order of priority. If it is not, changes will have to be made: tasks may change in order of priority, tasks may have to be delegated or delayed, or you may have to go to a higher authority and ask for help.

This planning and monitoring process can be seen in the diagram shown below.

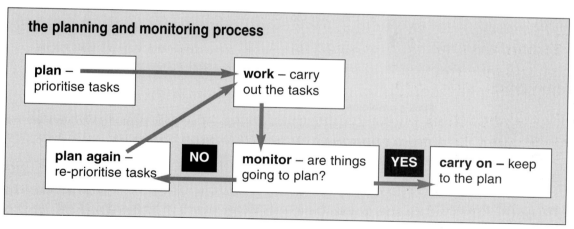

the planning and monitoring process

dealing with changed priorities

At the beginning of a working day you are likely to have a set list of tasks and priorities. You may have a 'To Do' list to work from and a diary for specific timed events. But all sorts of things can happen, but hopefully not at the same time:

- your colleague, who shares your work, is off sick, so you have twice as much paperwork to deal with as usual

- the post – which brings the bulk of the documents you have to process – does not arrive because of a postal strike

- your email system breaks down because there is a virus in the server

These situations call for tasks to be re-prioritised, for resources to be assessed, and for assistance to be called for. Your work plans will have to be changed, as we will see in the Case Study which follows.

FLICK'S DAY – CHANGING THE PRIORITIES

Flick works as an accounts assistant at the Liverpool head office of Estro PLC, a company that makes vacuum cleaners.

The Case Study which starts on page 100 showed how Flick prioritised her tasks on one working day – Thursday 6 February.

In this Case Study we will see how she copes with unexpected events on that day by changing the priorities of her tasks and asking for help from managerial staff where appropriate.

To recap on what Flick had planned for Thursday:

1   The urgent tasks were to provide the January sales figures for the Accounts Manager and to help with moving the computers in the afternoon.

2   Flick had planned to get some jars of office coffee at lunchtime.

3   There was the normal daily sales order processing work and filing to be done.

4   Flick also had to provide some customer activity printouts for the following day and had been asked to move some filing records.

Flick's problems

Flick was faced with a number of problems as soon as she got to work on the Thursday. These meant that her carefully thought out work plan was in trouble and would have to be revised. The problems were:

1   **09.30**. Her colleague, Kirsty, who helped her with her sales order processing work had to go home sick. She had eaten a dodgy curry the night before and was in no fit state to work. There was a trainee working on the invoicing as well, but Flick doubted if this trainee could cope with the extra work involved.

2   **10.00**. Flick saw from Kirsty's note that she had to give the Accounts Manager the January sales figures 'as soon as possible'. This seemed a bit vague. Did it mean during the morning, or would later in the day be OK?

3   **11.30**. Flick's printer jammed and a long run of invoices was ruined. She could not seem to get it to work again.

4   **12.00**. The Human Resources Manager phoned through to ask if she could 'pop in' to see her at 1.45. Was she free then? Flick knew that she had to move the computers at 2.00.

5   **12.30**. Flick realised that she was going to have to work for most of her lunch break. What about the coffee she was supposed to be getting?

Flick was faced with a number of situations which clearly meant that her work plan was going to be disrupted and would have to be revised. But how was she to do this? She obviously needed to make suggestions to the management about what should be done. Some of the decisions would have to be made by the management.

09.30 Kirsty away off sick

Kirsty's absence would mean that Kirsty's routine processing work would have to be done by someone else – either Flick (who was busy anyway) or the trainee – unless it could be left until the next day. Flick would need to assess how much work there was and then speak to the line manager, Josie. The line manager said to Flick 'Do what you can, concentrating on orders from the important customers. The rest will have to wait. I don't think the trainee can be left on her own yet.' Flick was not too happy about this because she was very busy herself. She would have to put some of her other tasks back in order of priority.

10.00 the figures for the Accounts Manager

Flick realised that this was a priority job. To clarify what 'as soon as possible' really meant, she emailed the Accounts Manager who replied that the figures would be needed by lunchtime that day for a meeting in the afternoon. This job remained top priority.

11.30 printer jam

The printer jam had to be referred to the line manager who called in the maintenance engineer. Flick knew that the invoices would have to be printed that day, so she arranged to print them on another printer through the network. She lost valuable time in sorting out this problem and only got back to work at 11.50, by which time she was getting really stressed.

12.00 Human Resources Manager

Flick realised that the 1.45 appointment with the Human Resources Manager would clash with having to move the computers. The request, however, came from a senior manager and took priority over most other tasks. Flick referred the problem to her line manager who said it would be OK for Flick to go to the appointment. Flick was secretly quite pleased to miss lugging the computers about.

12.30 coffee?

Flick realised that she would have to work through some of her lunch hour, which meant that she would not be able to get the coffee. She explained this to Jack, another colleague, who agreed to get the coffee for her.

17.00 end of the day review . . .

Flick is in good spirits because she has had a productive afternoon. Her work targets for the day have largely been completed, despite the changes of plan. The sales figures have been given to the Accounts Manager and much of the sales processing work has been completed. Flick has had an interview with the Human Resources Manager and even arranged for the coffee to be bought. How has this all been achieved? Flick has successfully reworked her priorities and made the most of her resources – delegating tasks and consulting higher authorities where appropriate.

WORKING IN ACCORDANCE WITH THE LAW AND REGULATIONS

When you work, you should always ensure that you are complying with the law and regulations that result from legislation – including European directives.

observing deadlines

Sometimes these laws and regulations will include deadlines that have to be met and planned for in the schedule of work. Examples of these include:

- **Company Annual Return**: under the Companies Acts limited companies have to complete an annual return form providing details about the company address, directors and shareholdings – a fine will result if the form is late.
- **VAT Return**: if a business is VAT registered, a VAT return (Form 100) has to be completed and sent off every quarter or year, normally with a repayment of VAT, within a month of the end of the VAT period – if it is late the business may end up with the VAT inspectors paying a visit.
- **Payroll**: a business has to send to the Inland Revenue the net tax and National Insurance collected through the payroll (if the payroll is monthly, the money has to be sent off by the 19th of the next month). A business also has to send off an annual payroll return (P35) in May.

observing copyright

The **Copyright, Designs and Patents Act 1988** states that written and electronic material must not – within certain limits – be copied for business or personal use. This particularly applies in the workplace to the use of the photocopier and the unauthorised copying of computer software. Copying music CDs is also illegal under the copyright laws! Work plans must therefore avoid copying resources, and funds must be made available, for example, for multiple copies of software.

observing equal opportunities

Employers must take great care these days with equal opportunities legislation in order not to discriminate in terms of sex, race, religion or age. Personnel planning must take this into account.

confidentiality

Employees always have to take care with confidentiality of information held both in paper records and also on computers (where secrecy is made easier through the use of passwords). For example, payroll information should always be kept strictly confidential and not revealed to other employees.

Also, information about customers and suppliers should never be revealed to outsiders. The only exception to this is in the case of banks who suspect customers of money laundering from drug dealing or funding terrorist activities. Here the law requires that the business *must* reveal information to the police authorities.

Data Protection Act

The **Data Protection Act (1998)** protects the confidentiality of information about individuals. It follows the guidelines of an EC Directive and brings the UK in line with European legal principles. The Act applies to:

- a filing system of records held on **computer** – eg a computer database of customer names, addresses, telephone numbers, sales details
- a **manual** set of accessible records – eg a card index file system of customer details

All organisations which process personal data should register with the Data Protection Commission. There are eight guiding principles set out in the Data Protection Act. These principles require that personal data is handled properly. They state that personal data must be:

1   fairly and lawfully processed

2   processed for limited purposes

3   adequate, relevant and not excessive

4   accurate

5   not kept for longer than is necessary

6   processed in line with the data subject's rights

7   kept securely

8   not transferred to countries outside the European Union unless it is adequately protected in those countries

The Data Protection Act requires that an organisation should not reveal, without permission:

- information about one customer to another customer
- information about its employees

retention of records

Business records are normally stored for at least six years (and a minimum of three years for payroll data). There are a number of legal reasons why financial data should be kept for this period of time:

- accounting records should be kept so that they can be inspected by the Inland Revenue if required (if there is a tax inspection)
- accounting records should be kept so that they can be inspected by HM Customs & Excise if required (if there is a VAT inspection)

Chapter Summary

- Employees in an organisation are encouraged to work together to achieve the objectives of the organisation.

- Employees are also required to work according to the established procedures of the organisation and also in line with their job descriptions.

- Tasks can be classified in a number of different ways – routine and non-routine, urgent and non-urgent, important and less important.

- Employees should acquire the skill of prioritising tasks according to these classifications and be able to plan their activities accordingly.

- A 'rule of thumb' order of priority for tasks is:

  1 urgent and important tasks

  2 urgent and less important tasks

  3 important and not urgent tasks

  4 tasks that are neither urgent nor important

  The second and third of these may be interchangeable, according to the context of the task.

- Employees should be familiar with different types of planning aids. They should be able to write their own 'To Do' lists and diaries. They should be able to understand complex planning aids such as project planning schedules and action plans, but it is unlikely they will have to draw them up.

- Employees should understand the need to monitor the progress of a work plan over time and have the flexibility to be able to re-prioritise if unexpected events happen.

- If priorities have to change, employees should be able to consult the appropriate higher authority if help is needed; they should also be able to delegate tasks if the need arises and the resources are available.

- Employees need to be aware of the legal restrictions on work practices. These are wide ranging and cover areas such as:

  – deadlines for forms and returns required by law, eg VAT Returns

  – copyright restrictions on photocopying and software copying

  – observing equal opportunities in the workplace

  – the need for confidentiality and observance of the Data Protection Act

  – the retention of records

Key Terms

objective	a goal towards which employees work, eg customer care, profitability
procedures	sets of instructions which dictate the way tasks should be carried out in an organisation
job description	a formal document issued by the employer setting out the extent of the tasks that an employee should carry out
routine task	a task which is part of the everyday work of an employee
non-routine task	an unexpected task which is not part of the everyday work of an employee
urgent task	a task which has a pressing deadline
important task	a task for which the employee is given specific responsibility and the completion of which significantly affects other employees
prioritising	deciding the specific order in which tasks should be carried out
'To Do' list	a checklist of tasks which can be ticked off when they are completed
planning schedule	a chart used for planning projects which organises tasks in terms of time and priority; it normally identifies the 'critical' tasks and allocates time for their completion
action plan	a checklist for a series of activities (normally for a project) which lists the main tasks consecutively by time period (eg monthly) and allocates responsibility and sets target dates for completion – it is very useful for monitoring progress
monitoring	the process of examining the progress of the work plan and re-prioritising tasks where appropriate
copyright	the legal protection given to written material and software designed to prevent illegal copying
equal opportunities	the legal protection for employees which helps to prevent workplace discrimination on the grounds of age, sex, race and religion
confidentiality	preventing personal records of employees and outsiders (on paper and computer file) falling into the hands of unauthorised people

Student Activities

7.1   What is the difference between a routine task and a non-routine task? Give examples of both from your own experience of the workplace. (If you have not been at work, ask family and friends).

7.2   Explain what is meant by the term 'prioritisation of tasks' and state why the process is necessary.

7.3   (a)   Define the difference between an urgent task and an important task.

   (b)   Normally an urgent task should be done before an important task. Give an example of a situation where the opposite may be true.

7.4   Give two examples of planning aids which are (or should be) commonly used by most employees in the workplace.

7.5   The eleven tasks below are examples of activities which a payroll assistant may have to carry out in an Accounts Department of a medium-sized company. It is Monday in the last week of the month and the office has just opened. Employees in the organisation are paid monthly, on the last day of the month, which is at the end of this week. The payroll has to be run through the computer on Monday and BACS instructions sent to the bank on Tuesday so that employees can be paid on Friday.

You are to reorganise the list, placing the tasks in order of priority.

- Look at the section diary and compare with your 'To Do' list.
- Send email to Marketing Department asking for monthly overtime figures to be sent through – they should have been received last Friday.
- Check that details of hours worked (including overtime) have been received from all departments.
- Distribute the departmental post.
- Draw up a notice advertising a staff trip out for next month.
- Process the hours of all the employees on the computer. Print out pay details and a payroll summary, including the schedule setting out the amount which will have to be paid to the Inland Revenue for income tax and National Insurance Contributions by 19th of the next month.
- Pass the payroll printouts to your line manager for checking, and when approved, print out the payslips for distribution.
- Put a note in the diary for the Inland Revenue cheque to be prepared on 5th of next month.
- Print out payroll statistics from the computer for your line manager – they are required for next week.
- Prepare the BACS payroll schedule for the bank to process on Tuesday.
- Pass the BACS payroll schedule to your line manager for checking.

7.6 *Note: this Activity can only be carried out after you have completed Activity 7.5.*

When you have prioritised your tasks in the payroll section, a number of events happen during the day which mean you might not be able to do all the work you had planned.

How would you react to the following situations? In each case explain what you would do and what the implications would be for your work plan for the day.

Remember that you can ask for help from colleagues or refer difficulties to a higher authority.

(a)   You get a call from Reception at 9.30, saying that your car in the car park has still got its lights on.

(b)   At 10.30 the Human Resources Manager calls to ask if you would like to sit in on a Quality Circle meeting at 14.00 to discuss Customer Service.

(c)   You get a call from reception at 11.30 saying that a friend has called and wants to talk on a personal matter.

(d)   When you are processing the email from Admin Department giving overtime hours, you notice that two employees are recorded as having worked 50 hours overtime. The normal maximum is 5 hours.

(e)   The computer system crashes, just as you are finishing processing the payroll.

7.7 Your work routine as an employee will be affected by various legal constraints. What type of legislation is involved in the following situations, and how would you deal with each request?

(a)   You are asked to arrange for the Annual Return of your company to be sent off.

(b)   You are asked to photocopy a section from a training book.

(c)   You are asked to set up a photo shoot of members of your workforce, who vary in sex, race and age. The picture will appear in a catalogue of your products.

(d)   A customer telephones and asks for the address and telephone number of another of your customers.

this chapter covers . . .

In this chapter we examine the importance of maintaining good working relationships with colleagues and the part played by effective communication and mutual respect and understanding between people in the workplace.

We explain the way in which a team should work together in order to achieve the objectives of the organisation, with team members helping and supporting each other to meet deadlines.

We also discuss how team work can go wrong, with conflicts breaking out and team members becoming dissatisfied with each other and the tasks in hand. Situations such as these can either be sorted out within the team, or they may need to be referred to a higher authority to provide a solution.

NVQ PERFORMANCE CRITERIA COVERED

unit 23   ACHIEVING PERSONAL EFFECTIVENESS

element 23.2

Maintain good working relationships

A   communicate with other people clearly and effectively, using your organisation's procedures

B   discuss and agree realistic objectives, resources, working methods and schedules and in a way that promotes good working relationships

C   meet commitments to colleagues within agreed timescales

D   offer assistance and support where colleagues cannot meet deadlines, within your own work constraints and other commitments

E   find workable solutions for any conflicts and dissatisfaction which reduce personal and team effectiveness

F   follow organisational procedures if there are difficulties in working relationships that are beyond your authority or ability to resolve, and promptly refer them to the appropriate person

G   treat others courteously and work in a way that shows respect for other people

H   ensure data protection requirements are followed strictly and also maintain confidentiality of information relating to colleagues

KNOWLEDGE AND UNDERSTANDING COVERAGE

5   *Work methods and practices in your organisation*

6   *Handling confidential information*

7   *Establishing constructive relationships*

8   *Why it is important to integrate your work with other people's*

13   *Maintaining good working relationships, even when disagreeing with others*

14   *The scope and limit of your own authority for taking corrective actions*

15   *Use of different styles of approach in different circumstances*

19   *Team working*

20   *Seeking and exchanging information, advice and support*

21   *Handling disagreements and conflicts*

22   *Showing commitment and motivation towards your work*

25   *Informing and consulting with others about work methods*

27   *Co-ordinating resources and tasks*

28   *The organisational and department structure*

29   *Own work role and responsibilities*

30   *Colleagues' work roles and responsibilities*

31   *Reporting procedures*

32   *Procedures to deal with conflict and poor working relationships*

TEAMWORK

what is a team?

Working with others implies the need for teamwork. It is easy to start to define a team by giving examples – a football team, a workplace team – and explaining that they work together – sometimes well and sometimes not quite so well. In the case of a football team this means that they sometimes lose.

But what exactly is a team?

A team is a group of people working together to achieve defined objectives.

In the case of a football team, the objective is clearly to play skillfully and defeat the other side. In the workplace a team can be a 'section group' working in one part of an office – eg a payroll section – or it can be a group working on a project, eg a group set up to improve customer service. The objective of a 'section group' will be to complete the work set efficiently, to a high standard and within the normal deadlines. The goal of a 'project group' will be to achieve the overall objective, eg an assessment of customer service and an overall improvement in standards.

benefits of teamwork

People working in a team often achieve better results than if they work on their own. The benefits include:

- **pooling of skills and abilities:** some people are better at some tasks and some are better at others, and so a team will take advantage of individual strengths and overcome individual weaknesses

the team at work

- **creative thinking:** working with other people means that individuals can be stimulated to create and share ideas on a scale that would probably not be possible if they were working on their own

- **motivation:** people get a 'buzz' out of working in a team – it gets people going and brings its rewards when the team is successful

- **help and support:** team members usually support each other when support is needed – this can take the form of advice, moral support and assisting with or taking over tasks which may be causing a problem

problems with teamwork

It should be pointed out, however, that teamwork is not always the simple answer to achieving objectives. Team members can sometimes be unco-operative and disruptive. When this happens, the other team members – and particularly the team leader – will have to sort out the situation, and if they are unable to do so, the problem will have to be referred to a higher authority. Problems with teamwork are covered later in this chapter (pages 124 to 126).

working at teamwork

Teamwork requires that team members are dedicated to achieving the team objective. This means that team members should:

- be committed to the work of the team

- understand their role in the team and the tasks they are allotted

- take full responsibility for what they do

- assume joint responsibility for the work of the whole team

- take note of and work to the schedules imposed by the team

COMMUNICATION AND TEAMWORK

The vital link between team members is **communication**. Although employees will communicate with outsiders – customers and suppliers, for example – it is the effectiveness of the internal communication channels which will make a significant difference to the success of teamwork. Communication channels include:

- oral communication – talking to people face-to-face
- oral communication – talking to people on the telephone
- written notes and memoranda
- fax
- email
- word-processed documents

We will describe the effective use of these communication methods in turn.

face-to-face oral communication

the importance of face-to-face communication

The time-honoured traditional method of communication is speech. This involves not just the words, but the body language and the tone of voice used. In the workplace this can take a number of forms:

- talking to and discussing work matters with colleagues informally
- passing on messages
- giving instructions
- taking part in informal and formal meetings
- interviews

Whole books have been written on the subject of communication skills and body language, but the basic guidelines for effective oral communication are:

- think about what you are going to say before you say it
- say it clearly and in an appropriate tone of voice
- look at the person (or people) you are speaking to and try to look positive and as if you mean what you are saying
- think 'body language' – do not yawn and look out of the window!
- try to make sure that what you have said has been understood by asking the person (people) involved
- listen to what is said in reply – and make notes if necessary

oral communication – the telephone

no need to worry about facial expressions on the telephone!

The same principles apply as for face-to-face communication, but remember that when speaking on the telephone you cannot rely on body language and facial expressions to convey your meaning, unless, of course, you have a video telephone. It is important when speaking on the telephone to:

- identify yourself and make sure that you know to whom you are speaking
- if you are taking an external call you will need to comply with your 'house style' for replying – the type of ringing tone in most organisations will tell you if this is the case
- speak extra clearly – remembering that the tone of your voice will compensate for the body language that will be missing

written notes and memoranda

Flick - Accounts Manager wants January sales figures by lunchtime today!

Kirsty 6 Feb 9.30

You can also communicate with team members using written **notes** and memoranda. Post-it notes or formal in-house notes are very useful in passing messages on – telephone messages received and reminders, for example. The important elements on a note are:

- the name of the person the note is for
- the name of the person the note is from
- the date and time
- the message, setting out clearly and concisely what is required

The **memorandum** ('memo') is a formal note used within an organisation. It can be addressed to one individual, or copied to members of a team. The use of the memorandum nowadays is on the decline as internal email becomes more popular.

MEMORANDUM

To   John Stone, Finance Manager

From   Tim Blake, Sales Manager   **Ref** TB/AC/1098

Copies to n/a   **Date** 23 June 2003

Subject Bad payers

Please can you let me have an updated list of our customers who exceed their credit period and pay late. By Friday 27th please. Thanks.

electronic communication – fax

The fax (short for 'facsimile') enables you to transmit electronically an exact copy of the details on a sheet of paper. This can either be done on a computer or on a fax machine. If you use a fax machine you feed the sheet into the machine, dial up the recipient on the inbuilt telephone pad and transmit the document down the line. The machine at the other end will print out an exact copy of the original document.

If you are sending a fax externally – a copy invoice to a customer, for example, you normally send a 'fax header' first sheet and then feed in any further pages/documents as required. If the fax is internal you can just send an A4 sheet with a note written on it, or whatever you need to communicate – it could be a map of how to get to a client's premises.

electronic communication – email

Email is the sending and receiving of electronic messages by means of computer. Emails can be:

- external – communications with customers through the internet, or

- internal – through a network of computers in the business – an intranet

Emails can be sent quickly and cheaply within the UK and overseas.

When someone wants to check an email account, it is necessary to log in. A list of messages is displayed. The user can read them or delete them. When a message is read, it is easy to reply to it. The original message re-appears and comments can be added to the original. If a message is of interest to someone else, it can be forwarded. Computer files – eg spreadsheets – can also be sent by email as 'attachments'.

When composing an email, a screen such as the one illustrated below is used.

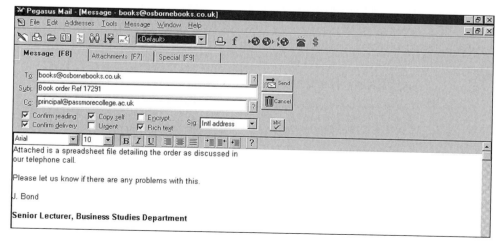

word-processed documents

Word-processing programs are now common in the workplace. They are used for producing a wide variety of written documents, often in a set 'house style'. Standard letters and memos can easily be produced from template files set up on the computer.

Mail-merge facilities enable a word-processed letter file to import names and addresses from a computer database file and print out a batch for sending out. Word-processing programs can produce documents with sophisticated page layouts and tables; they can also import graphics and embody colour elements for illustrative purposes.

If you are working in a team – in an everyday work situation or a project team – you may well use a word-processing package for:

- letters and memos (see illustration of a memo below)
- internal forms and stationery
- order forms for customers
- meeting agendas
- meeting minutes
- notices to team members
- formal reports

You will no doubt be able to think of other ways in which word-processing is used in the workplace.

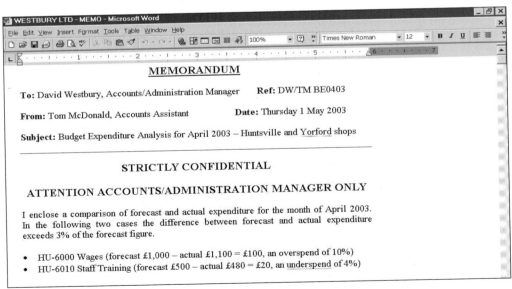

For further details of communication methods and formats, please refer to the Osborne Books *Foundation Accounting Tutorial*, Chapter 8.

CREATING GOOD WORKING RELATIONSHIPS

what does a team need?

Remember that a team at work can be a group – a section – which works together on a daily basis, or it can be a special project team set up for a specific and limited purpose. A team needs to establish for itself:

- **objectives** – eg a level of quality in the case of a 'section' team, a specific result in the case of a project team
- levels of **resources** – people, equipment, time, money
- a definition of **working methods** – deciding how the work is to be carried out, and by whom
- **schedules** – time targets for specific tasks

In the case of a work 'section' team these factors will be based on current practice, and will be refined over time, improved perhaps by regular team meetings to discuss the way the team works.

In the case of a 'project' team, the team members will sit down and plan out all these factors at the start of the project.

types of team member

If you have worked in any form of team, you will know that there are many different types of character that can make up that team:

- the leader – who may be a natural leader, appointed by the group, or who may be an employee appointed to a position of responsibility
- an ideas person who provides inspiration to the group
- the steady worker who gets things done
- the slacker and complainer who does not get things done and causes problems
- the person who provides moral and practical support to others when problems arise

ideal qualities of a team member

In order to create good working relationships, as a team member you should ideally:

- be pleasant and polite to other team members
- be prepared to co-operate, even if you do not agree with everything that is decided
- respect the opinions of others and be prepared to listen to what others have to say

- ask others if you need help and be prepared to help others if they need it
- avoid backbiting and criticising the leader behind his/her back
- keep confidences – if information is not to be released, you should keep quiet about it (this is also a requirement of the Data Protection Act)

This probably sounds all very theoretical and ideal. In the Case Study on page 126 we examine how this works in practice. First, however, we must also explain what can go wrong in working relationships, and how those problems can be resolved.

DEALING WITH PROBLEMATIC WORKING RELATIONSHIPS

what can go wrong?

Problems are often caused by disagreements. These disagreements can either be resolved within the team, or exceptionally they may have to be referred to a higher authority. There are two main causes of disagreement:

- **the nature of the work** itself and the way it is carried out – for example a new line manager joining the team with very different ideas about how the work should be tackled
- **personal conflicts** within the group – clashes of personality types, even extending to bullying and other forms of harassment

Very often the two areas combine to produce a problem which can be very difficult to sort out. Look at the illustration below which shows what can irritate other people at work and cause problems in working relationships.

causes of breakdowns in working relationships

I do not like people who are . . .
- inefficient
- inflexible
- rude
- over-critical
- over-sensitive
- sexist

I do not like people who have . . .
- an inflated opinion of themselves
- personal hygiene problems

sorting out disagreements within a team

It is important for team members to resolve problems in working relationships themselves, within the dynamics of the team, if that is possible.

If the problem is simply one which relates to **the work itself** – for example procedures for the processing of sales orders – it could be sorted out by informal discussion between team members (ie work colleagues) and then referral to a higher authority.

If the problem is one which relates to a **personal conflict between team members** – for example 'she's too slow at her work, and always on the phone to her boyfriend' or 'he's a real pain to work with because he's always making insulting remarks' – the problem should be sorted by other means, for example:

- observing other people dealing with that person – do they have the same problems?
- talking it over with other members of the team – do they think the same way, or is it just you getting things out of proportion?
- talking to the person involved – do they actually realise how they affect other people?

If there really is a problem – and it's not just you being negative or over-sensitive – then the matter should be raised with a higher authority.

taking the matter further – grievance procedures

If the working relationship problem is actually one of harassment – for example bullying or someone making passes at you – the matter should definitely be raised with a higher authority. If it is the line manager who is the cause of the problem, the matter should be referred to a more senior authority.

If the matter is very serious, the **grievance procedure** can be adopted. A **grievance** is a complaint against the employer. Grievances can include:

- unfair treatment by managers – for example, being passed over for promotion because of gender or race; unfair dismissal (an extreme case!)
- unfair pay – men paid more than women for the same work

All employers must have a written grievance procedure. This will be set down in writing and made available to all employees. It will state:

- the person to whom the employee must go to with their complaint – often a chat with the employee's line manager (as we saw above) will be enough to sort matters out.
- if the employee is still not happy with the way they are being treated they will be allowed to make a formal complaint to a senior manager, or even to a director

- if the employee is still not happy with the result, they may then have to go outside the organisation and take the matter to an Employment Tribunal (an independent informal court)

If the employee is a Trade Union member, the Union will be able to give advice and support in every stage of the process. The Union will also give support in the case of a disciplinary procedure.

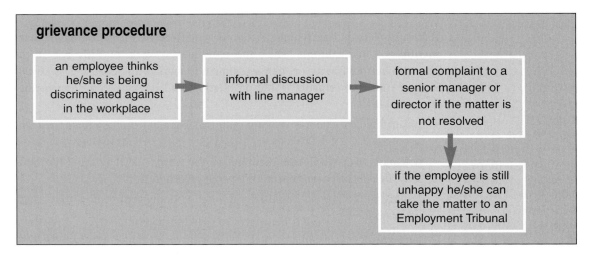

grievance procedure

an employee thinks he/she is being discriminated against in the workplace → informal discussion with line manager → formal complaint to a senior manager or director if the matter is not resolved → if the employee is still unhappy he/she can take the matter to an Employment Tribunal

We will now look at a Case Study which shows how working relationships are developed within a work team, and the way in which problems can be resolved.

Case Study

WORKING ON RELATIONSHIPS

situation

The accounts staff of Hermes Limited, which sells motor accessories, have been asked to provide sales information for the Marketing Department. The team from the Accounts Department is headed up by Jen, a line manager. She will be helped by two accounts assistants, Tom and Jacqui.

Jen is a line manager, an organiser, experienced at her work and respected by staff.

She can sometimes be intolerant of people who do not seem to know what they are doing.

She is also old-fashioned and sexist, preferring to have female assistants, claiming privately that they are quicker and more accurate at their work than male assistants.

Tom *is a mature and experienced accounts assistant, a hard worker, accurate and with an eye for detail.*

He is not as fast as some assistants, but he can be relied upon to keep to deadlines.

He is also ready to help others when they need assistance. He has a quiet personality, but is popular in the office.

Jacqui *is a confident accounts assistant, always ready to give her opinion on how to get things done.*

She is sometimes inaccurate because she tends to work too quickly.

She is capable of achieving her targets, however, when given help and encouragement.

the project

The Accounts Department has been asked by the Marketing Department to provide regular monthly statistics relating to customer sales. The requirements are:

1   sales by product and unit

2   sales by product and sales value (£)

3   the percentage of sales (in £) analysed into:
    - customers who buy on credit
    - cash sales
    - e-commerce (credit card/debit card sales from the company's website)

4   total sales (£) for each of the top 20 credit customers

This will require

- the analysis of sales figures extracted from the company's computer accounting system
- the setting up of spreadsheets to analyse the data
- the setting up of a monthly report template on a word-processing program – this will include charts imported from the spreadsheet program

the meeting

Jen calls a meeting of her team to discuss how they are going to set up this system and maintain it to produce the monthly statistics.

They decide the following:

objective — the objective is to provide regular monthly sales statistics for the Marketing Department

resources
- two assistants (Tom and Jacqui)
- computers and computer time
- data held on the computer and in manual records
- assistance and monitoring from line manager (Jen)

work scheduling
- Tom, who has good IT skills, is to work on the spreadsheets and the report format. He will then help Jacqui input the data into the spreadsheets and extract the report
- Jacqui is to extract the data held on the computer accounting system and some manual records
- Jen will monitor and supervise the whole process with regular meetings

deadlines
- 2 weeks for Tom to complete spreadsheets and Jacqui to extract the data
- 2 further weeks for transferring data to the spreadsheets and producing the first report
- total time allowed 4 weeks

what actually happened

Week 1

At the end of the first week Jen calls a meeting to monitor progress on the project. Tom has worked to schedule and has prepared the spreadsheets set up to process the statistics. Jacqui has fallen behind in extracting the data, which means that Tom has insufficient test data to input. Jen says, laughing 'Don't worry, Jacqui will soon catch up, she is a good quick worker, like all the girls in this office.' Tom keeps silent about this sexist remark.

Week 2

During week 2 Tom finds out that Jacqui's data is incomplete and inaccurate. He offers to put it right for her, so that he can ensure that the data for the spreadsheets will be accurate. Jacqui is happy to accept Tom's assistance. Tom also completes the word-processed report template.Tom knows that the deadline is important, because if the project falls behind, the Marketing Department will not get their figures on time.

At the end of the second week Jen calls a meeting to monitor progress. She is pleased with progress and jokingly remarks to Jacqui that things are going well and that Jacqui 'must have given Tom a helping hand.' Tom is very angry about this but says nothing.

Weeks 3 and 4

During the final two weeks, Tom and Jacqui are scheduled to work together to complete the project, and it is during these two weeks that problems occur.

Tom resents the fact that he has to help Jacqui to meet the deadlines, but what really annoys him is that Jen does not recognise his effort, but in fact makes sexist remarks at his expense.

Tom has two problematic working relationships – and neither of them are really his fault: he has to work extra hard to make up for Jacqui's shortcomings and he has to deal with discrimination from his superior.

So what are Tom's practical alternatives?

1   Tom can refuse to help Jacqui.

2   Tom can complain to Jen about Jacqui's inaccuracy.

3   Tom can complain to a more senior manager about Jen's sexist remarks.
    or . . .

4   Tom can carry on as he always has done and do more than his fair share of the work and try to ignore the sexism of his line manager, Jen.

the solution

Tom decides to chat to his mate Dave about these problems.

the Jacqui problem

Dave suggests that Tom talks to other colleagues to see how they deal with Jacqui, but in the end he thinks Tom will have to accept the Jacqui situation as there will always be people at work who work less hard than their colleagues. Tom will certainly get no backing from Jen. If Tom refuses to help Jacqui, he is being unco-operative and is not helping the development of good working relations. The Jacqui problem is clearly one Tom will have to sort out himself.

the Jen problem

Dave points out that the sexist remarks made by Jen will be very annoying and hurtful, but unless Tom can produce any firm evidence of sexual discrimination in the workplace, he cannot bring any formal complaint against his line manager and start the grievance procedure.

Dave suggests that if Tom considers that his chances of promotion are being affected by reports given by Jen, he should talk to his departmental manager or to a Human Resources manager.

Dave also suggests that Tom takes the initiative and talks to Jen herself about the situation. This may not be the most obvious solution, but it may be that Jen does not realise that by making sexist remarks she is damaging a valuable working relationship. It may be that she thinks she is being funny. A frank and reasoned discussion with Jen may help to change Jen's attitude.

The 'right' solution to the Jen problem is far from clear. But as with the Jacqui problem, the solution is one that Tom will have to work out for himself. In the meantime he has his deadlines to meet and the project to complete . . .

Chapter Summary

- Effective teamwork is needed if a group of employees is to achieve its objectives.

- The benefits of teamwork include: the pooling of skills and abilities, the opportunity for creative thinking, motivation within the team, help and support from team members.

- Communication is important for the effective functioning of a team. Communication methods include: oral (face-to-face and telephone), notes and memoranda, faxes, email, word-processed documents.

- Teams can be normal day-to-day working groups, or they can be special project teams set up for specific purposes.

- When working in a team it is important that each member should be polite, co-operative, respectful of others, helpful, loyal and discreet.

- Working relationships within a team can go wrong, either because of the work itself, or because of a breakdown in the relationship – or both.

- When working relationships within a team do go wrong, they should ideally be resolved within the group. If that is not possible, they may have to be resolved by a higher authority using the grievance procedure.

Key Terms

team	a group of people working together to achieve defined objectives
oral communication	communication involving the spoken word – either face-to-face or telephone
written communication	communication involving writing – including notes and memoranda
electronic communication	communication involving electronic transmission of data – including faxes and emails
grievance procedure	the formal procedure to follow when you have a complaint against your employer
Employment Tribunal	an independent informal court which decides cases relating to employment problems

Student Activities

8.1 Explain the meaning of the term 'team' and outline the benefits of working in a team.

8.2 State the objectives of the team in which you work (or a team in which a friend or family member works).

8.3 List the methods you (or friend or family member) use to communicate with colleagues during a working day. In each case state what type of message is involved.

8.4 Write down the six qualities a team member should ideally possess to enable the team to function effectively.

Optional task: give yourself a score out of ten for each quality, add up the total score and convert to a percentage. How do you think you have done? How do you compare with your colleagues? How could you improve your teamwork skills?

8.5 A new colleague, Jake, has just joined your team, and you find him to be an absolute pain – he thinks he knows everything, and doesn't. He also talks about colleagues and the line manager behind their backs.

What action could you take to deal with a character like Jake?

8.6 Jasmina, a friend of yours, has worked in a payroll section for a number of years. She has a poor working relationship with her line manager, Tim, and as a result has been passed over for promotion a number of times. The line manager has been heard to say 'There's no point in promoting her and giving her all the extra training, she wants to have a baby, and may well leave the firm when it suits her.'

What practical advice can you give Jasmina about dealing with her working relationship with the line manager?

In this chapter we examine the need for you to formulate and put into action a plan of self-improvement. This can involve the type of work you are already carrying out in the workplace, it can also involve career planning, ie investigating the type of work you would like to do in the future. Self-improvement involves a number of stages:

- taking stock of your current work activities
- thinking about how you could develop your work activities and further your career
- investigating the ways in which you could acquire new skills and knowledge – by going on work training courses, taking qualifications, reading, surfing the internet
- reviewing your performance and progress from time-to-time to see how you are getting on

If you are not in employment, the same principles apply to your acquiring skills and knowledge which may help you get a job.

NVQ PERFORMANCE CRITERIA COVERED

unit 23   ACHIEVING PERSONAL EFFECTIVENESS

element 23.3

Improve your own performance

A   identify your own development needs by taking into consideration your current work activities and also your own career goals

B   define your own development objectives and, where necessary, agree them with the appropriate person

C   research appropriate ways of acquiring new skills and knowledge

D   ensure that development opportunities are realistic and achievable in terms of resources and support from relevant persons

E   review and evaluate your performance and progress and also to agreed timescales

F   monitor your own understanding of developments relating to your job role

G   maintain and develop your own specialist knowledge relevant to your own working environment

H   undertake learning that will help you improve your performance

WHY THIS CHAPTER IS DIFFERENT

This chapter is rather different from the other chapters in this book in that it is more loosely structured. It is intended as a series of guidance notes and hints rather than a formal 'lecture'. It is hoped that it will prove useful in helping you both with your career and with your accounting studies.

The diagram below shows you where you should be heading.

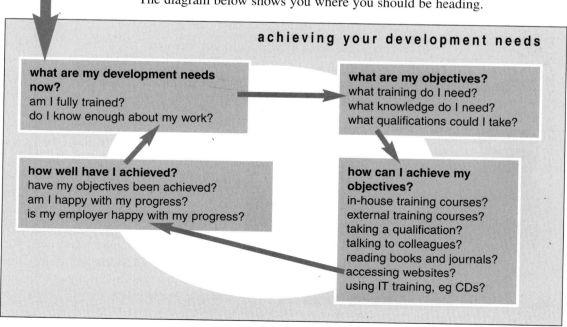

achieving your development needs

what are my development needs now?
am I fully trained?
do I know enough about my work?

what are my objectives?
what training do I need?
what knowledge do I need?
what qualifications could I take?

how well have I achieved?
have my objectives been achieved?
am I happy with my progress?
is my employer happy with my progress?

how can I achieve my objectives?
in-house training courses?
external training courses?
taking a qualification?
talking to colleagues?
reading books and journals?
accessing websites?
using IT training, eg CDs?

In order to improve your **performance** and career prospects – your **development needs** – you need to take stock of your current position and identify exactly where it is you want to go. The diagram on the bottom of the previous page shows a process which involves four stages:

1   what are my development needs now?

2   what are my objectives?

3   how can I achieve my objectives?

4   how well have I achieved?

The process, of course, is continuous and subject to continual review.

We will look at each of the four stages in turn.

WHAT ARE MY DEVELOPMENT NEEDS NOW?

You may be in employment at present, or it is possible that you are not in work. Whatever the situation, you will need to take a look at what your personal development needs are. You need to carry out a form of personal 'audit' of your **knowledge** (what you know) and **skills** (how you put it into practice). How do you do this? You need to ask yourself a number of questions and also talk them over with colleagues. You will see that a number of the following questions can apply to people who are not in work:

1   Am I content with what I am doing at present?

2   Am I confident that I have the background knowledge for what I am doing at work?

3   Do I need further training for what I am doing at work?

4   Do my skills need developing? For example, do I need to go on a spreadsheet course? Do I need to improve my selling skills?

5   Where do I see myself working in a year's time?

6   Where do I see myself working in five year's time?

talk it over at your appraisal interview

If you are at work you may well discuss these issues on a regular basis with your management as part of the **appraisal** process. At the interview, objectives should be set, training needs identified and promotion prospects explored. You should always be given the opportunity of discussing with management how you can develop your **skills** and **knowledge** and improve your performance in the workplace.

WHAT ARE MY OBJECTIVES?

When you have thought about your development and career needs, and discussed them with others, you will be in a position to set specific objectives – targets – for achievement. These will not be vague and woolly like 'I want to be a manager' or 'I want to be better at my work' but will be very specific. For example you might say that within the next twelve months . . . .

'I need to learn more about spreadsheets because they are used a lot in the Accounts Department.'

'I need to learn more about the Sage computer accounting system. I can do the basics, but haven't a clue about doing journal entries. I don't really know my debits from my credits!'

'I'd like to do an accounting qualification – there seems to be a lot of opportunity in that area.'

'I need to know more about the theoretical background to the accounting work I am doing at the moment.'

HOW DO I ACHIEVE MY OBJECTIVES?

The objectives need to be made very specific. One reason for this is that your employer may have to book and arrange things for you. For example:

'I need to go on an advanced Excel spreadsheet course at the local Training Centre so that I can process the Sales data and produce charts for management.'

'I need to work alongside Kulvinder for a week so that I can learn more about operating our Sage computer accounting system.'

'I want to enrol on an NVQ course in accounting at the local college because I want to be promoted within the department.'

'I need to read that Osborne Books accounting textbook recommended by my colleague because it will give me the background knowledge I need.'

You may well already have identified the fact that what this person really needs to do is to enrol on an AAT (or equivalent) course at the local college. This will provide the theoretical and practical background to a career in an accounts office and also help with promotion prospects, as will be seen in the Case Study on the next page.

HOW WELL HAVE I ACHIEVED?

The process of personal planning never stands still. As in any planning process, achievement will have to be monitored on a regular basis, eg every twelve months at the annual appraisal interview when both the employer and the employee will need to re-assess the situation. The planning process can then start all over again – new objectives, new targets, a new action plan.

In the Case Study which follows we look at the personal planning carried out by a typical accounting employee/student.

Case Study

MAKING THE MOST OF YOUR RESOURCES

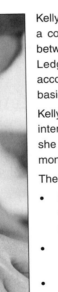

Kelly works in the Accounts Department of CompLink Limited, a computer supplies wholesaler. She moves to some extent between the sections, but spends most of her time in Sales Ledger, where she processes orders on the computer accounting system, checks documentation and has started basic work in Credit Control, sending out statements.

Kelly wants to get on in her job and career. At her appraisal interview in the Summer, she agreed with her Manager that she should achieve certain targets within the next twelve months.

These objectives included:

- in-house training in the Accounts Department, achieved by work-shadowing (working alongside a colleague in Credit Control)
- an intensive two day training course in computer accounting at a local external training provider
- enrolment at the local college to take an AAT Foundation Accounting course, which runs from September to the following June when she will have to sit an Exam

What resources can Kelly call upon to help her in her training and studies?

colleagues

Kelly can talk to her colleagues and make the most of their experience and knowledge, picking up tips about dealing with procedures and situations. This is particularly useful in Credit Control where Kelly can learn how to deal with slow payers - interpreting all their lame excuses about not paying (eg 'the cheque has been signed, but we haven't sent it yet' or 'we don't seem to have received the invoice'). She will also learn how to interpret the Aged Debtors Analysis and to send out the appropriate letters without offending the 'important' customers who invariably pay late.

college

Studying accounting is never an easy option, but Kelly finds that having a good teacher and a lively class helps her understand the more difficult areas of the course. She is able to ask questions about the areas she finds difficult and is given help when her trial balance doesn't balance.

textbooks

Kelly uses the Osborne Books range of accounting texts and finds that they help her understand difficult concepts and prepare well for her Exam and Skills Tests. She is online at home and finds the Student resources on the publisher's website a help (www.osbornebooks.co.uk)

other websites

The AAT website (www.aat.org.uk) is full of useful information and links. Its Student Forums provide bulletin boards where students can post queries about study topics, and then receive replies. The website of the AAT's magazine (www.accountingtechnician.co.uk) also contains useful resources, including revision articles, reviews and job adverts.

Chapter Summary

- Improving your own performance involves a number of stages, starting with you assessing what you do at work (if you are in work) and thinking about where you want your career to take you.

- You should then set defined objectives (targets). If you are at work this is best done with your employer – possibly in an appraisal interview.

- You should then work out how you are going to achieve these objectives, assessing the resources you are going to need. The extent of these will depend whether or not you are at work: you may consider tapping into the expertise of your colleagues, training in-house and externally, taking a qualification, obtaining study material in various media.

- The final stage in the personal development process is to review and evaluate your progress and to establish new targets and action plans. If you are at work, this may be carried out with your employer as part of the appraisal process.

Key Terms

development needs	the opportunities for improvement in your personal knowledge and skills which will help further your career (or start it, if you are not in work)
objectives	specific targets for development needs
knowledge	what you need to know to enable you to do a job at work
skills	the ability to put knowledge into practice
appraisal	the process whereby an employer interviews an employee on a regular basis, assessing past performance and identifying development needs
performance	your success rate in achieving your development needs

Student evidence collection

Note

The full guidance for producing the evidence you need for this element is set out on pages 199 to 218.

In order to prepare for this you should be considering how you can carry out your personal 'audit' – ie assess your current position and consider the knowledge and skills you will need to develop your performance and career. This exercise is equally valid, whether you are in employment or not.

Answers to student activities

CHAPTER 1: COMPUTER SYSTEMS AND SOFTWARE

1.1 Hardware comprises the computer equipment and software the computer programs.

1.2 An intranet is an internal website which operates through a network and enables employees to share data, documents and internal web pages. An intranet cannot be accessed by outsiders.

The internet is a telephone link to an internet service provider which gives access to the world wide web (www).

Advantages of an intranet are improved communication within the organisation, the ability to share information and to access internal web pages.

1.3 (a) See text page 12

(b) See text page 13

(c) See text page 14

(d) See text page 17

(e) See text page 18

1.4 The visual checklist should be in numbered form and include checking of hardware components (central processing unit and peripherals), power plugs, peripheral connections, safety of cabling.

1.5 (a) A system password enables you to gain access to the computer itself – to 'log on'. A software password enables you to gain access to individual programs on the computer.

(b) Passwords are necessary for security reasons. The system password prevents access to the system from intruders and other unauthorised people. A software password restricts access to individual programs from individual unauthorised employees, eg access to personnel records.

1.6 A variety of back-up policies could be quoted – for example the use of a 'one disk per working day' system or a rotation of any practical number of disks. Mention should be made of where the disks are to be stored, eg there could be two sets, one stored securely on the premises, another off-site. Mention could also be made of sending data by email to a remote location as a method of backing up smaller files.

1.7 Paper out – normally fixed by the operator.

Paper jam – can be fixed by the operator, although assistance may be needed in more serious cases.

Toner out – assistance would normally be needed.

Software problem – the printer refuses to print or prints out nonsense – assistance would definitely be needed.

Mechanical breakdown – assistance would definitely be needed from an engineer.

CHAPTER 2: DATA SECURITY

2.1 The passwords should be:

- six characters long

- easily memorised

- accompanied by explanations of the source of the password elements and the reasons why nobody could guess them

2.2 (a) It is possible that the colleague is trying to work out your password in order to gain unauthorised access to the data. You should report the fact that the password may be insecure to your line manager, who is then likely to arrange for it to be replaced.

(b) Illegal copying of software is a breach of copyright and unacceptable. You should point this out to your colleague.

(c) The attachment could contain a virus and should not be opened. The matter should be reported to your line manager.

(d) The colleague should be advised to move the disks as overheating could damage them and lead to file corruption and loss of data. This could be serious if the disks are the only current back-up.

(e) This is a matter of health and safety and is covered by the Display Screen Equipment Regulations. It sounds as if your colleague is spending too long at the keyboard and may have a problem with posture and eyesight. You should mention the fact that the employer has responsibilities to the employee, including the giving of work breaks, a free eyesight test and suitable seating. You should suggest that your colleague in the first instance should speak to the line manager to discuss the problem.

(f) This is a question of confidentiality, and the employer is regulated by the Data Protection Act. It would be a breach of this Act if you gave information about one customer to another customer without authorisation, particularly if the answer might give a bad impression of the customer's credit rating. You should politely decline the request to give the information.

CHAPTER 3: WHO IS RESPONSIBLE FOR HEALTH AND SAFETY?

3.1   Both employer and employee.

3.2   A hazard is something that could harm you. A risk is a measurement of how likely it is that you will be harmed by a hazard.

3.3   (a)   Health and Safety at Work Act 1974.

      (b)   -   ensure health, safety and welfare of employees

           -   provide a Health and Safety Policy Statement (where there are five or more employees)

           -   allow the appointment of a safety representative

      (c)   -   take reasonable care of own health and safety

           -   take reasonable care of the health and safety of others

           -   cooperate with the employer or anyone acting on his or her behalf to meet health and safety requirements

3.4   (a)   Control of Substances Hazardous to Health (regulations affecting the identification and storage of hazardous substances).

      (b)   Reporting of Injuries, Diseases and Dangerous Occurrences (regulations requiring the official reporting of these events).

      (c)   Health and Safety Executive (the body responsible for the regulation, control and inspection of health and safety in the workplace).

3.5   (b)

3.6   (a)   Emptying of bins is the employer's responsibility. If bins are not emptied the rubbish could become a hazard for two reasons: it could trip somebody up if it spills onto the floor; it could be a health hazard if there is rotting food in it.

      (b)   A drink on top of a computer is the responsibility of the employee and should be avoided at all costs; the hazard is a spill which could damage the electronic components of the computer beyond repair.

      (c)   It is the employer's responsibility to provide adequate seating; in the case of a computer workstation this means an adjustable seat. This avoids the hazard of bad backs and other muscular disorders.

      (d)   It is the employee's responsibility to use the furniture and equipment provided in an appropriate way. The hazard here is that the employee may fall off the chair or strain a muscle or damage the spine.

CHAPTER 4: WHO DEALS WITH THE HAZARDS?

4.1 The hazard here is a safety one. The danger is that the fire alarm could be going off because there actually is a fire, and the priority would then be to get everyone out alive, invoices or no invoices. As far as the options are concerned:

(a) This is just untrue and should be avoided at all costs.

(b) This is true, and while possibly getting your colleague into trouble, you would be alerting the employer to the fact that fire safety regulations are not being observed. If there was a fire you would possibly be saving her life. This is the correct option.

(c) This is avoiding the issue entirely and shirking the employee's responsibilities for health and safety. The result would be that the employer would be unaware of breaches of fire safety regulations. This could prove fatal in the event of an actual fire.

4.2 The hazard here concerns security. The danger is that employees or even outsiders could obtain confidential information from the computer. Bank details may be on the computer and obtained for fraud. Addresses could also be obtained for purposes of harassment. Details of pay could be obtained and be a cause of unrest at work ('he's earning £2,000 more than me and he's useless' etc). The answer here is less clear cut and could lead to some interesting discussion:

(a) This is avoiding the issue and shirking the employee's responsibilities for security in the workplace. The result would be that the employer would be unaware of breaches of security.

(b) This is arguably the correct option in this situation if your colleague is at the same level of seniority as yourself. If he fails to log off next time or on subsequent occasions, option (c) would then become the course of action.

(c) See (b). If your colleague is junior to yourself it would be more appropriate to advise the line manager who can then check out the position and take action.

4.3 It is possible that Trish is a serial whinger and inefficient at her work, but ...

(a) Her employer is potentially liable for:

- a possibly substandard monitor - it flickers and is difficult to read
- not varying Trish's work sufficiently
- possibly requiring her to work for long periods of time without a break
- stressing her by telling her to hurry up

(b) Trish is responsible for her condition to the extent that:

- her posture is poor, despite the chair being appropriate for the job
- her work area is poorly organised and a mess
- it is possible that she does not take breaks when she has the opportunity
- she may need to get her eyes tested, or may have neglected to do so when offered a test

Your advice to Trish could be to talk to her employer about her symptoms, having regular breaks, arranging eye tests, the need to improve the quality of the screen, and the lack of variation of the work (could she be trained to do something else as well?).

She could also talk to her union rep who may give her a copy of the HSE leaflet 'Working with VDUs' - or she could download it from www.hse.gov.uk

You could also tactfully mention the importance of good posture and organisation of her work area.

CHAPTER 5: ACCIDENTS AND EMERGENCIES

5.1   Five from:

- name of Safety Officer
- name of First Aider(s)
- location of First aid box
- location of Accident Book
- emergency procedures
- types of fire extinguisher

5.2   (a)   Percy. Placing a mug of coffee on top of a computer is negligent on his part.

(b)   Explain to Percy his own responsibilities for Health & Safety in the office – including where not to put mugs of hot coffee. Also mention the likely need to replace the keyboard.

(c)   A light scald is not a reportable injury under RIDDOR. As Percy is likely to come back to work the next day, the 'over three day' situation will not arise.

(d)   Circulation of a note about employee responsibility for Health & Safety in the office, mentioning specific instances such as mugs of hot coffee on computers.

(e)   The form should give full details of the circumstances of the accident, the injury, the action taken by the First Aider and the further action of communicating employee responsibility for Health & Safety to the office staff.

5.3   • death or major injury in the workplace – giving examples of major injuries

- 'over three day' injuries where the employee is away from work for more than three days for less serious injuries

- dangerous occurrences which could have resulted in injury, but did not, giving examples of dangerous occurrences

5.4   (a)   Water. Most effective for paper. Powder would work, but much messier.

(b)   Carbon Dioxide. Powder would work but would ruin computer irretrievably.

(c)   Powder. The only choice as it deals with all substances.

5.5   See text in the bottom half of page 76, together with selected points from the bottom section of page 77. The meeting point should be mentioned by name.

CHAPTER 6: MANAGING YOUR WORK AREA

6.1 An <u>effective</u> working environment is one which will result in the achievement of the objectives of the organisation. An <u>efficient</u> working environment is one in which the organisation achieves the required results with the minimum wastage of resources.

6.2 (a) Three from: tidy, clean, everything in its place, everything accessible, VDU correct, chair correct

     (b) Examples such as not being able to find a document when user is absent, user not being able to find document when present, user not passing on data needed by someone else, user not passing on message because message lost, data disk corrupted because of dirt etc. The implications on effectiveness (task not being done) and efficiency (time/money wasted) should be discussed in each case.

6.3 The list is a very personal choice and could include pictures, posters, postcards, photos, 'toys', fruit, holiday souvenirs etc etc.

     (a) Most items would normally be allowed, subject to the sensitivities of colleagues and management. Colleagues are likely to object to items that make a noise or smell. Female colleagues might object to men bringing in girlie calendars or pictures. Management would object to items that get in the way of the work processes, eg very large plants, personal stereos etc.

     (b) The appearance of an office that is open to public view would be strictly controlled by the employer. Any personal items would have to be unobtrusive, eg small photos, and wallspace is likely to be used for advertising or promoting corporate identity. Any public areas would have items welcoming to the public, eg flowers, appropriate magazines.

6.4 (a) You would have to consult your colleagues first, and then your employer. Remember that it will be noisy (affecting colleagues) and will use power (which will increase the electricity bill).

     (b) An oil heater under a desk would be a fire hazard and totally unacceptable. You would need to bring to the employer's attention the fact that the 15 degree temperature is below the legal minimum of 16 degrees for an office. It would then be up to the employer to adjust and increase the level of the heating.

     (c) This is a common problem and would need to be decided among the employees, particularly bearing in mind the feelings of the people nearest to the window (and the noise).

     (d) A flickering fluorescent light would need to be referred to a line manager, who should arrange for it to be replaced.

6.5 (a) You should fill up the paper tray.

     (b) You should try to clear the jam, following the manufacturer's instructions. If you are unsuccessful, consult a senior assistant.

     (c) Refer to a senior assistant. This is a skilled and potentially messy job.

     (d) This is unauthorised copying. The answer should be 'no'.

(e)   This is not for you to question, and you should do it. You may think it is unauthorised, but the line manager may be doing some research connected with work.

(f)   This is copyright material and should not be copied. Sometimes you are allowed to copy short extracts from copyright material, but two chapters is not a short extract.

(g)   You will need to use the reducing function on the machine. The instructions are on the top panel (see illustration on page 90).

(h)   This flashing symbol is the Periodic Maintenance light. It should be referred to the line manager.

CHAPTER 7: PLAN AND ORGANISE YOUR WORK

7.1   A routine task is a task which is part of the everyday activity of the workplace. A non-routine task is an unexpected task. Examples should be given as appropriate.

7.2   Prioritisation of tasks is deciding on the order in which the tasks should be completed.

7.3   (a)   An urgent task is a task which is required to be done by a specific deadline; an important task is a task for the completion of which an employee is given personal responsibility.

(b)   The situation where the urgent task is relatively unimportant.

7.4   'To Do' list, diary.

7.5   A suggested order for the list:

1   Distribute the departmental post.

2   Look at the section diary and compare with your 'To Do' list.

3   Check that details of hours worked (including overtime) have been received from all departments.

4   Send email to Marketing Department asking for monthly overtime figures to be sent through – they should have been received last Friday.

5   Process the hours of all the employees on the computer. Print out pay details and a payroll summary, including the schedule setting out the amount which will have to be paid to the Inland Revenue for income tax and National Insurance Contributions by 19th of the next month.

6   Pass the payroll printouts to your line manager for checking, and when approved, print out the payslips for distribution.

7   Prepare the BACS payroll schedule for the bank to process on Tuesday.

8   Pass the BACS payroll schedule to your line manager for checking.

9   Put a note in the diary for the Inland Revenue cheque to be prepared on 5th of next month.

10   Print out payroll statistics from the computer for your line manager – they are required for next week.

11   Draw up a notice advertising a staff trip out for next month.

7.6   (a)   You should go and turn the lights off as soon as an opportunity arises. It will not take long and will prevent the battery going flat.

   (b)   This should be referred to your line manager. You are very busy, but the line manager should decide whether you should go – it may be possible for the line manager to delegate your work to someone else.

   (c)   The friend should be told politely that you cannot speak during working hours. You could suggest a lunch-time meeting.

   (d)   This looks like an obvious error, or even a fraud! You cannot take action yourself, but should refer the matter to your line manager to take action.

   (e)   The work will have to be redone as a matter of urgency. The computer will have to be rebooted and the data re-input (to the extent that it has not been saved). If there are further problems, the line manager will have to be alerted and technical assistance requested.

7.7   (a)   Companies Act. The Return should be sent off by the deadline.

   (b)   Copyright law. The photocopying may be illegal and should be refused.

   (c)   Equal opportunities. The workforce seen in publicity material should be representative of the employees in terms of race, sex and age.

   (d)   Data Protection. This would be a breach of confidentiality and should be refused.

CHAPTER 8: WORKING WITH OTHERS

8.1   A team is a group of people working together to achieve defined objectives. The benefits of working in a team include: the pooling of skills and abilities of different team members, creative thinking stimulated by group discussion, motivation from working with others, the help and support provided by other team members.

8.2   The answer will depend on the circumstances involved.

8.3   See the communication methods described on pages 119 to 122. It is important that each method listed should be accompanied by some form of analysis – ie is the method formal or informal? How does it suit the type of message being conveyed?

8.4   A suggested six (note that these are not prescriptive):

   1   being pleasant and polite

   2   being cooperative

   3   listening to and respecting the opinions of others

   4   asking for and providing help

   5   do not backbite

   6   keep confidences

8.5 The important point here is to make sure that your objection to Jake is based on issues which relate to the work itself rather than your personal (and possibly subjective) reaction to him. You should:

- Observe the ways in which the other members of the team deal with him – do they also have problems? If they do not, the problem may lie with you.

- Talk the problem over with the other team members – do they think the same way?

- Talk the matter over with Jake, if you feel you are able to.

If it emerges that the problems with Jake extend to the whole team and the standard of work and workplace efficiency is being affected, there may be a case for taking the matter to a higher authority.

8.6 Jasmina's problem is one of possible sexual discrimination, although the evidence is circumstantial rather than actual. (It may be, of course, that she is hopeless at her work.) She should in the first instance talk the matter over with the line manager, stressing her wish for promotion and motivation, making it clear that she intends to carry on working if she starts a family. If the line manager cannot come up with a satisfactory explanation for keeping her where she is, she should take the matter to a Human Resources Manager (or equivalent). If she has firm evidence of sexual discrimination, she may have grounds for starting the grievance procedure.

CHAPTER 9: IMPROVING YOUR PERFORMANCE

There are no answers for this chapter. The Student Activity is to prepare for obtaining Portfolio evidence.

Unit 21
Working with computers

Simulation: Pronto Supplies Limited
for Level 2 students

- This assessment is based around a tried and tested 'set up and go' set of computer accounting exercises, using Sage Line 50 software.

- Evidence produced by these exercises covers in full the assessment requirements of Unit 21 (see next page for mapping of performance criteria).

- The Evidence produced also covers the computer accounting requirements of the Range for Units 1, 2, 3 and 4 (see page 151 for mapping).

- This Assessment should ideally be carried out when Units 1, 2, 3 and 4 have been covered in full.

- Sage set-up and back-up files are available direct from Osborne Books, either by email, or on disk. Please call 01905 748071 for details.

- The accounting data and tasks in this Assessment may also be used or adapted by Centres who do not run Sage accounting software.

Unit 21
performance criteria mapping

element	coverage	tasks
21.1	A perform initial visual safety checks and power up the computer system	1
	B use passwords to gain access to the computer system where limitations on access to data is required	1,25
	C access, save and print data files and exit from relevant software	throughout
	D use appropriate file names and save work	throughout
	E back up work carried out on a computer system to suitable storage media at regular intervals	1,25
	F close down the computer without damaging the computer system	1
	G seek immediate assistance when difficulties occur	25
21.2	A ensure passwords are kept secret and changed at appropriate times	25
	B ensure computer hardware and program disks are kept securely located	25
	C identify potential risks to data from different sources and take steps to resolve or minimise them	25
	D maintain security and confidentiality of data at all times	25
	E understand and implement relevant legal regulations	25

Units 1, 2, 3 & 4
performance criteria mapping

element	coverage		tasks
UNIT 1			
1.1	Range	Computerised coding, computerised day books, computerised statements	2-5 7
1.2	Range	Computerised cash book and ledgers	13,17
	K&U 15	Operation of a computerised accounting system, including output	2-8
UNIT 2			
2.1	Range	Computerised coding, computerised day books, computerised ledgers	9-12
2.2	Range	Computerised cash book, petty cash book and ledgers	14,18,19,20
	K&U 16	Operation of a computerised accounting system, including output	9-12
UNIT 3			
3.1	Range	Computerised cash book and ledgers and bank reconciliation statement	21
3.2	Range	Computerised journal, sales ledger control account and non-trade debtors control account	22,6,23
	K&U 9	Operation of a computerised accounting system, including output	8,12,22
UNIT 4			
4.2	Range	Word processed report	24
	K&U 7	Methods of analysing information in spreadsheets	24
	K&U 8	Methods of presenting information in word processed documents	24
	K&U 18	House style for presentation of word processed documents	24

Assessment Tasks

IMPORTANT NOTE ABOUT SOFTWARE

using Sage?

The tasks in this Assessment are based on the use of Sage Line 50 software by a computer supplies company, Pronto Supplies Limited.

The Sage file (Company.25) for setting up the business, its customers and suppliers and 'main' ledger accounts on the computer system is available to Centres from Osborne Books. Please call 01905 748071 for details.

Research by Osborne Books has shown that Sage is a popular choice in Centres, and it is hoped that the provision of a Sage 'set up' file for Pronto Supplies will save Centres a great deal of work in setting up the Assessment.

Practical explanations of the use of Sage software are contained in Chapters 25 to 28 of Osborne Books' 'Foundation Accounting Tutorial'. The chapters are based on the Pronto Supplies Limited business and show how the tasks in the Assessment should be tackled. They are therefore important background reading if Sage software is being used.

You will probably be familiar with the requirement for the non-trade debtors control account (eg for rents receivable) from the NVQ Standards. This rather unusual item cannot be set up in Sage, which requires all debtor accounts to be controlled through the standard Debtors Control Account (1100 in 'Nominal'). This Assessment instead requires the setting up of a special Rents Receivable Account as a Sales Account, which can then monitor rent as it is received by the business.

not using Sage?

This Assessment has been designed so that Centres not using Sage software will be able to use the data in the tasks in order to obtain the required evidence.

ASSESSMENT SCENARIO

the business

Pronto Supplies is a limited company run by Tom Cox who has worked as a computer consultant for over ten years.

Pronto Supplies provides local businesses and other organisations with computer hardware, software and all the other computer 'bits and pieces' such as disks and ink cartridges needed in offices. It also provides consultancy for computer set-ups through its proprietor, Tom Cox. Pronto Supplies has eight employees in total. The business is situated on an industrial estate, at Unit 17 Severnvale Estate, Broadwater Road, Mereford, Wyvern, MR1 6TF.

the accounting system

Pronto Supplies Limited started business on 1 January 2001. The business is registered for VAT (ie it charges VAT on its sales) and after a month of using a manual accounting system Tom has decided to transfer the accounts to Sage Line 50 software and sign up for a year's telephone technical support.

Tom has chosen Sage Line 50 because it will enable him to:

- record the invoices and credit notes issued to his customers to whom he sells on credit
- record the invoices and credit notes issued by his suppliers
- pay his suppliers on the due date
- keep a record of his bank receipts and payments
- enable him to record petty cash transactions
- record his income and expenses, business assets and loans in a main (nominal) ledger

looking after the computer system

Tom realises that he will have to take steps to manage his computer system so that:

- it works efficiently on a day-to-day basis and the hardware and software does not fail
- the data in the system is kept secure and is backed up on a regular basis

To help train his staff, Tom has set up a 'start of day' and 'end of day' checklist to cover issues such as checking the computer equipment, power and peripheral leads on arrival and shutting down and backing-up properly at the end of the day.

SUMMARY OF TASKS

Tasks	Activity
1	system checks
2-8	selling to customers on credit
9-12	buying from suppliers on credit
13-16	dealing with credit payments
17-18	dealing with cash receipts and payments
19-20	operating a petty cash system
21	bank reconciliation statement
22	journal entries
23	setting up a rents receivable account
24	using a spreadsheet and a memorandum to report sales figures
25	preparing a word processed guide for the operation of a computer system

TASK 1: SYSTEM CHECKS

Tom has produced the checklist shown below and on the next two pages for the visual checks and other routines his staff have to carry out. The checks should be made when the staff start up the computer system on arrival in the morning and when they close it down at the end of the day. You are to:

* carry out the same checks when you operate your computer system
* sign and date each check
* provide the information where requested and make any comments if appropriate

If any checks do not apply to your system, you should state 'N/A' in the comments box and give an appropriate reason.

CHECK	Hardware components in place and properly connected?
Date	
Signature	
Comments	

CHECK	Computer system plugged into mains and power on?
Date	
Signature	
Comments	

CHECK	Internet access plugged in (if appropriate)?
Date	
Signature	
Comments	

CHECK	Equipment and cabling complying with Health & Safety Regulations?
Date	
Signature	
Comments	

CHECK	Use password to enter computer system
Date	
Signature	

State whether system is standalone or networked ....

Comments

CHECK	Use password to access software
Date	
Signature	
Comments	

CHECK	Backing-up your work on close down
Date	
Signature	

What data storage medium do you use for your back-up? ....

Comments

CHECK	Close down
Date	
Signature	

What procedures did you carry out to close down the computer system safely?

If you had to leave the computer system running when you had finished your work, what procedures did you carry out with the software and hardware?

TASKS 2-8: SELLING TO CUSTOMERS ON CREDIT

technical note
Before starting these inputting tasks you should ensure that the Sage file 'Company.25' (provided by Osborne Books) is loaded onto your computer.

Task 2

Making sure that you have set the program date to 9 February 2001 (SETTINGS menu), enter the invoice details from the batch sheet below into the computer.

Check your totals before saving and print out a Day Books: Customer Invoices (Summary) Report to confirm the data that you have saved. Retain the printout.

BATCH SHEET

SALES INVOICES ISSUED

invoice	name	date	details	net amount	VAT
10023	John Butler & Associates	5/02/01	1 x 17" monitor	400.00	70.00
10024	Charisma Design	6/02/01	1 x printer lead	16.00	2.80
10025	Crowmatic Ltd	6/02/01	1 x MacroWorx software	100.00	17.50
10026	Kay Denz	8/02/01	2 hours consultancy	120.00	21.00
Subtotals				636.00	111.30
Batch total					747.30

Task 3

Enter the following credit note batch details into the computer.

Check your totals before saving and print out a Day Books: Customer Credits (Summary) Report to confirm the data that you have saved. Retain the printout.

BATCH SHEET

CREDIT NOTES ISSUED

credit note	name	date	details	net amount	VAT
551	David Boossey	6/02/01	Software returned	200.00	35.00
552	French Emporium	6/02/01	Disks returned (hardware)	40.00	7.00
Subtotals				240.00	42.00
Batch total					282.00

Task 4

It is now a week later and the date is now 16 February 2001. Change your program date setting (SETTINGS menu).

You have a further batch of invoices to process.

Enter the details into the computer. Check your totals before saving and print out a Day Books Summary Report to confirm the data that you have saved.

account	invoice date	number	details	net	VAT
John Butler & Associates	12/02/01	10027	2 hours consultancy	120.00	21.00
David Boossey	13/02/01	10028	1 x EF102 printer	200.00	35.00
French Emporium	14/02/01	10029	1 x QuorkEdit software	400.00	70.00
L Garr & Co	16/02/01	10030	2 x Zap drive	180.00	31.50
Jo Green Systems	16/02/01	10031	1 x Fileperfect software	264.00	46.20
Prism Trading Ltd	16/02/01	10032	1 x 15" monitor	320.00	56.00

Task 5

You also on the same date have two credit notes to process. Enter the details into the computer. Check your totals before saving and print out a Day Books Summary Report to confirm the data that you have saved.

account	date	reference	details	net	VAT
Jo Green Systems	12/02/01	553	1 x printer lead	16.00	2.80
Mendell & Son	13/02/01	554	Zap disks (hardware)	20.00	3.50

Task 6

You have been asked to prepare an Aged Debtors Analysis. Run a debtor analysis report (as at 16 February) from REPORTS in Customers. Compare the total balance on the report with the Debtors Control Account balance. Print a Nominal Activity Report for Debtors Control Account.

Task 7

Your customer David Boossey asks you for a statement of account as at 16 February.

Either print out a statement (account DB001) from CUSTOMERS, which could be faxed, or email the statement and keep a printed copy of the email (your tutor will provide you with an email address).

Task 8

Print out a Trial Balance as at 16 February 2001 to show the balances of the Nominal (Main) Ledger.

The figures should agree with the Trial Balance shown on the next page.

Pronto Supplies, trial balance as at 16 February 2001

Pronto Supplies Limited
Period Trial Balance

To Period: Month 2, February 2001

N/C	Name	Debit	Credit
0020	Plant and Machinery	35,000.00	
0030	Office Equipment	15,000.00	
0040	Furniture and Fixtures	25,000.00	
1100	Debtors Control Account	47,666.70	
1200	Bank Current Account	12,450.00	
2100	Creditors Control Account		32,510.00
2200	Sales Tax Control Account		18,242.70
2201	Purchase Tax Control Account	26,600.00	
2300	Loans		35,000.00
3000	Ordinary Shares		75,000.00
4000	Computer hardware sales		86,040.00
4001	Computer software sales		15,564.00
4002	Computer consultancy		2,640.00
5000	Materials Purchased	69,100.00	
6201	Advertising	12,400.00	
7000	Gross Wages	16,230.00	
7100	Rent	4,500.00	
7103	General Rates	450.00	
7200	Electricity	150.00	
7502	Telephone	275.00	
7504	Office Stationery	175.00	
	Totals:	264,996.70	264,996.70

TASKS 9-12: BUYING FROM SUPPLIERS ON CREDIT

Task 9

Set the program date to 16 February 2001. Enter the following invoice details into the computer. Check your totals before saving and print out a Day Books: Supplier Invoices (Summary) Report to confirm the data that you have saved.

PURCHASES INVOICES RECEIVED					
invoice	name	date	details	net amount	VAT
11365	Delco PLC	9/02/01	Desktop computers	3,600.00	630.00
8576	Electron Supplies	9/02/01	Peripherals	2,000.00	350.00
2947	MacCity	12/02/01	Powerbooks	2,400.00	420.00
34983	Synchromart	14/02/01	Software	1,280.00	224.00
Subtotals				9,280.00	1,624.00
Batch total					10,904.00

Task 10

Enter the following credit note details into the computer. Check your totals before saving and print out a Day Books: Supplier Credits (Summary) Report to confirm the data that you have saved.

CREDIT NOTES RECEIVED					
credit note	name	date	details	net amount	VAT
7223	Delco PLC	6/02/01	1 x Computer	480.00	84.00
552	MacCity	8/02/01	1 x optical mouse	38.00	6.65
Subtotals				518.00	90.65
Batch total					608.65

Task 11

On the same day Tom receives two further supplier invoices in the post. He wants them to be input straightaway while the computer is up and running. He checks all the documentation and finds that the invoices are both correct. You are to input them, taking care to use the correct nominal code (0030 for Office Equipment). The computer and printer purchased are not for resale to customers but are to be used as office equipment at Pronto Supplies. When the input is complete the totals should be checked and a Day Book Summary Report printed (showing just the last two invoices, if possible).

invoice	name	date	details	net amount	VAT
11377	Delco PLC	14/02/01	Desktop computer	400.00	70.00
8603	Electron Supplies	14/02/01	Laser Printer	360.00	63.00
Subtotals				760.00	133.00
Batch total					893.00

Task 12

When you have completed tasks 9 to 11, print out a trial balance dated 16 February 2001.

Also run and print out an Aged Creditors Analysis from Reports in Suppliers to show the position of the Purchases Ledger as at 16 February 2001.

Check your trial balance against the figures shown below. If they agree, your input is correct.

Pronto Supplies, trial balance as at 16 February 2001

Pronto Supplies Limited
Period Trial Balance

To Period: Month 2, February 2001

N/C	Name	Debit	Credit
0020	Plant and Machinery	35,000.00	
0030	Office Equipment	15,760.00	
0040	Furniture and Fixtures	25,000.00	
1100	Debtors Control Account	47,666.70	
1200	Bank Current Account	12,450.00	
2100	Creditors Control Account		43,698.35
2200	Sales Tax Control Account		18,242.70
2201	Purchase Tax Control Account	28,266.35	
2300	Loans		35,000.00
3000	Ordinary Shares		75,000.00
4000	Computer hardware sales		86,040.00
4001	Computer software sales		15,564.00
4002	Computer consultancy		2,640.00
5000	Materials Purchased	77,862.00	
6201	Advertising	12,400.00	
7000	Gross Wages	16,230.00	
7100	Rent	4,500.00	
7103	General Rates	450.00	
7200	Electricity	150.00	
7502	Telephone	275.00	
7504	Office Stationery	175.00	
	Totals:	276,185.05	276,185.05

TASKS 13-16: RECEIPTS FROM CUSTOMERS AND PAYMENTS TO SUPPLIERS

Task 13

Set the program date to 28 February 2001. Enter the following customer cheques into BANK (CUSTOMER). Use the reference 'cheque'.

Print out a Day Books: Customer Receipts (Summary) Report from REPORTS in BANK. Agree the day book total with the batch total (below) to confirm the accuracy of your input.

John Butler & Associates	£5,500.00
Charisma Design	£2,400.00
Crowmatic Limited	£3,234.00
David Boossey	£3,165.00
French Emporium	£5,553.00
Jo Green Systems	£3,461.20
L Garr & Co	£8,500.00
Mendell & Son	£4,276.50
Prism Trading Limited	£2,586.00
Batch total of payments received	£38,675.70

Task 14

Enter the following cheques Tom is paying to suppliers into the computer (SUPPLIER in BANK). If you are able, print remittance advices for each payment. Print out a Day Books: Supplier Payments (Summary) Report from REPORTS in BANK. Agree the day book total with the batch total (below) to confirm the accuracy of your input. The cheques are dated 28 February.

Delco PLC	£5,186.00	Cheque 123001
Electron Supplies	£8,500.00	Cheque 123002
MacCity	£4,455.35	Cheque 123003
Synchromart	£7,600.00	Cheque 123004
Tycomp Supplies	£6,160.00	Cheque 123005
Batch total of payments made	£31,901.35	

Task 15

If you have not already allocated your credit notes, check through your customer accounts by opening up the Customer Receipts screen for each one. You may find that some of them have a credit note outstanding and an invoice which has not been completely paid. You should in each case allocate the credit note to the appropriate invoice. Ensure in each case that the correct bank account is selected before you make the adjustment.

Task 16

Repeat the procedure in Task 15 by opening up the Supplier Payments screen for each supplier. You should in each case allocate the credit note to the appropriate invoice.

TASKS 17-18: DEALING WITH CASH RECEIPTS AND PAYMENTS

Task 17

Ensure the program date is set at 28 February 2001. Enter the following bank cash receipts into the computer. Check your totals before saving and print out a Day Books: Bank Receipts (Summary) Report to confirm the accuracy of your input.

Date	Details	Nominal code	Net amount (£)	VAT (£)	ref.
9 Feb 2001	Hardware sales	4000	12,500.00	2,187.50	10736
9 Feb 2001	Software sales	4001	4,680.00	819.00	10737
16 Feb 2001	Hardware sales	4000	15,840.00	2,772.00	10738
16 Feb 2001	Software sales	4001	3,680.00	644.00	10739
23 Feb 2001	Hardware sales	4000	17,800.00	3,115.00	10740
23 Feb 2001	Software sales	4001	4,800.00	840.00	10741
	Totals		59,300.00	10,377.50	

Task 18

Keep the program date as 28 February 2001.

Enter the following cash payments into the computer. Take care over the nominal accounts that you choose and the VAT Tax codes used. T1 is the standard rate code, T2 is for exempt items and T9 is the code for transactions which do not involve VAT.

Check your totals before saving and print out a Day Books: Bank Payments (Summary) Report.

Date	Details	Nominal code	Net amount (£)	VAT (£)	chq no
12 Feb 2001	Materials purchased	5000	15,500.00	2,712.50	122992
14 Feb 2001	Advertising	6201	10,200.00	1,785.00	122993
15 Feb 2001	Furniture	0040	5,000.00	875.00	122994
16 Feb 2001	Rent	7100	4,500.00	787.50	122995
19 Feb 2001	Rates	7103	350.00	exempt	122996
23 Feb 2001	Electricity (RPower)	7200	158.00	27.65	122997
26 Feb 2001	Telephone (ZipTelecom)	7502	310.00	54.25	122998
26 Feb 2001	Stationery	7504	340.00	59.50	122999
28 Feb 2001	Wages	7000	16,780.00	no VAT	123000
	Totals		53,138.00	6,301.40	

TASKS 19-20: OPERATING A PETTY CASH SYSTEM

Task 19

Keep the program date as 28 February 2001. On 1 February Tom cashed cheque 122991 for £100 at his bank to set up a petty cash system. Carry out a bank transfer from Bank Current Account to Petty Cash Account for this amount.

Task 20

Keep the program date as 28 February 2001. Tom has authorised five petty cash vouchers (shown below and on the next page). Input these, taking particular care with the VAT element on each one (postages are VAT exempt and stationery is standard-rated).

Print out a Day Books: Cash Payments (Summary) Report to confirm the accuracy of your input of the five vouchers. Hint: remember to select the Petty Cash Bank account on the screen before running the report.

petty cash voucher		Number *PC101*
	date	*7 Feb 2001*

description		amount	
		£	p
Stationery		36	00
	VAT	6	30
Receipt obtained		42	30

signature ..... *Nick Vellope* .....

authorised ..... *Tom Cox* .....

petty cash voucher		Number *PC102*
	date	*14 Feb 2001*

description		amount	
		£	p
Postages		25	00
	VAT		
Receipt obtained		25	00

signature ..... *R Patel* .....

authorised ..... *Tom Cox* .....

petty cash voucher

Number *PC103*

date *20 Feb 2001*

description		amount	
		£	p
Stationery			
	VAT		
Receipt obtained (includes VAT)		18	80

signature *B Radish*

authorised *Tom Cox*

---

petty cash voucher

Number *PC104*

date *28 Feb 2001*

description		amount	
		£	p
Postage stamps		5	00
	VAT		
Receipt obtained		5	00

signature *R Cook*

authorised *Tom Cox*

---

petty cash voucher

Number *PC105*

date *28 Feb 2001*

description		amount	
		£	p
Stationery			
	VAT		
Receipt obtained (includes VAT)		4	70

signature *R Patel*

authorised *Tom Cox*

TASK 21: BANK RECONCILIATION STATEMENT

Keep the program date as 28 February 2001.

Tom has an online facility with his bank and has just printed out his bank statement as at 28 February. He decides to carry out a bank reconciliation on the computer, using the RECONCILE function through BANK.

The starting balance of the bank statement is £12,450, which agrees with the balance of account 1200 'Bank Current Account' on the computer, as shown on the opening trial balance. The closing balance of the bank statement is £35,522.45.

All the items on the computer screen (see below) are on the bank statement apart from cheque 123005 for £6,160 which has not yet gone through the bank account.

When you have completed the reconciliation process, SAVE and run and print out a 'Bank Report: Reconciled and Un-reconciled' to show the items that have been reconciled and any that have not.

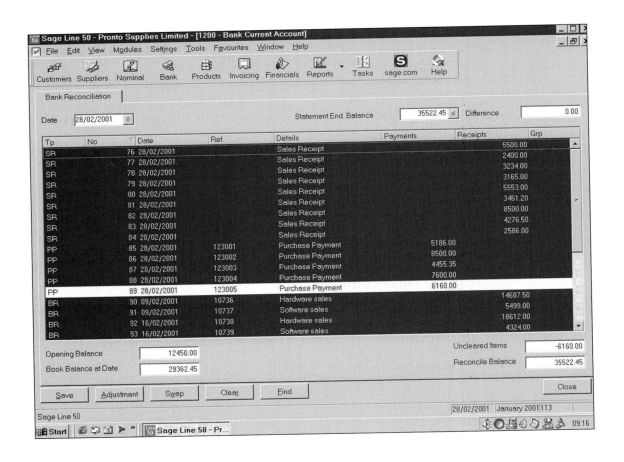

TASK 22: JOURNAL ENTRIES

Keep the program date as 28 February 2001.

Tom has been talking to his accountant about the categories of expenses which are recorded in his Nominal (Main) Ledger. He finds that a payment of £100, made on 20 January, which appears under advertising (account 6201) was actually for office stationery (account 7504).

The accountant suggests that Tom makes a journal entry to adjust the position, debiting account 7504 and crediting account 6201.

Make an appropriate journal entry, using the same VAT code (T1) as on the original transaction. The reference is 0041 and the current date 28 February 2001. The details are 'wrong post 20/01/01'. The JOURNALS screen is accessed through NOMINAL.

Print out a Day Books: Nominal Ledger Report dated 28 February 2001 from REPORTS in NOMINAL and check the details to confirm the accuracy of your input.

Print out a Trial Balance as at 28 February 2001 and check it against the Trial Balance on the next page.

TASK 23: SETTING UP A RENTS RECEIVABLE ACCOUNT

Change the program date to 6 March 2001.

Tom has decided to let out two small offices in his building. He asks you to set up a control account in NOMINAL to record the money owed by the two tenants.

You look into the ways of doing this but find that Sage does not allow you to set up a separate control account for non-trade debtors, as all debtor accounts are controlled and monitored through Debtors Control Account 1100.

You suggest instead to Tom that you set up a separate sales account for rents received. In this way you will be able to monitor the amount of rent income you receive, while at the same time keeping an eye on the tenant accounts in the main Sales Ledger. Any aged debtors report produced will soon point out any slow payment or non-payment of rent.

You are to:

- email a message to Tom explaining the situation and making the recommendation explained above (your Tutor will provide you with an email address)

- print out and retain a copy of your email

- set up a new account called 'Rents Receivable' – the account number allocated will be 4003

- when the account is set up, select account 4003 on the NOMINAL screen and print out a Nominal List Report which will show that you have opened the account

Pronto Supplies Limited

Period Trial Balance

To Period: Month 2, February 2001

N/C	Name	Debit	Credit
0020	Plant and Machinery	35,000.00	
0030	Office Equipment	15,760.00	
0040	Furniture and Fixtures	30,000.00	
1100	Debtors Control Account	8,991.00	
1200	Bank Current Account	29,362.45	
1230	Petty Cash	4.20	
2100	Creditors Control Account		11,797.00
2200	Sales Tax Control Account		28,620.20
2201	Purchase Tax Control Account	34,577.55	
2300	Loans		35,000.00
3000	Ordinary Shares		75,000.00
4000	Computer hardware sales		132,180.00
4001	Computer software sales		28,724.00
4002	Computer consultancy		2,640.00
5000	Materials Purchased	93,362.00	
6201	Advertising	22,500.00	
7000	Gross Wages	33,010.00	
7100	Rent	9,000.00	
7103	General Rates	800.00	
7200	Electricity	308.00	
7501	Postage and Carriage	30.00	
7502	Telephone	585.00	
7504	Office Stationery	671.00	
	Totals:	313,961.20	313,961.20

TASK 24: USING A SPREADSHEET AND MEMORANDUM TO REPORT SALES FIGURES

Tom asks you to compare his sales figures for the first two months of the year against the budgeted figures for Pronto Supplies Limited. The results are as shown in the table set out below.

The sales figures are divided into the three categories of computer hardware, computer software and computer consultancy.

	Budgeted sales for Jan/Feb (£)	Actual sales for Jan/Feb (£)
Computer hardware	125,000	132,180
Computer software	25,000	28,724
Computer consultancy	5,000	2,640

You are to:

- Format a suitable spreadsheet for the three columns of the table shown above, adding a fourth column showing the difference between the budgeted and actual figures for each of the three categories of sales.

- Add a further row to the spreadsheet to show the totals of the three money columns.

- Print out and retain a copy of the spreadsheet.

- Word process a memorandum report to Tom, setting out the spreadsheet data as a table and reporting the differences between budgeted and actual sales.

  Use your own name.

  Ensure that you use the accepted 'house style' for the memorandum report (check with your tutor to see what this involves).

TASK 25: GUIDELINES FOR OPERATION OF A COMPUTER SYSTEM

Tom is pleased with the work you have been doing, and knowing that you are studying for your first year of the NVQ Accounting course, he asks you to write a short guide to the operation of the company's computer accounting system. The object of this task is to provide the background knowledge needed by employees joining the company.

Tom would like the guide to be word processed and set in sections as shown below.

Each section should be headed up as indicated and use should be made where possible of bold text, underlined text, bullet points and tables.

1   Passwords
- why are passwords used and how are they kept secret?
- how does the business restrict access to certain types of computer data?
- when does the business need to change passwords?

2   Security
- how can computer hardware be kept secure?
- what are the risks to computer software and how can it be protected?
- what are the risks to computer data – eg corruption, theft, illegal copying, breaches of confidentiality – and how can they be avoided?

3   Back-up policy
Describe the data back-up system of the company.

4   Legal background
What laws and regulations affect the operation of a computer system? For example:
- Health & Safety (including VDU regulations)
- software copyright
- protection of personal data
- retention of documents

5   Getting help
What can go wrong with a computer system? For example:
- hardware breakdown
- software failure
- data corruption

What should done and whom should be contacted when something goes wrong?

Unit 21
Working with computers

Simulation: Anne Field Enterprises
for direct entry Level 3 students

- This assessment is designed for use by students who have started their NVQ studies at Level 3.

- Evidence produced by these exercises covers in full the assessment requirements of Unit 21 (see next page for mapping of performance criteria).

- Part of the evidence generated – a spreadsheet and a report – is produced as part of the Portfolio work for the compulsory Unit 7 'Reports & Returns', covered in Osborne Books' 'Costing & Reports Tutorial'.

  This evidence is required by Unit 7 Knowledge and Understanding items:

  13 tabulation of accounting and other quantitative information using spreadsheets

  14 methods of presenting information: written reports; diagrammatic; tabular

  This Portfolio evidence should be cross-referenced as appropriate.

Unit 21
performance criteria mapping

element	coverage		tasks
21.1	A	perform initial visual safety checks and power up the computer system	1
	B	use passwords to gain access to the computer system where limitations on access to data is required	1,5
	C	access, save and print data files and exit from relevant software	3,4
	D	use appropriate file names and save work	3,4
	E	back up work carried out on a computer system to suitable storage media at regular intervals	1,5
	F	close down the computer without damaging the computer system	1
	G	seek immediate assistance when difficulties occur	5
21.2	A	ensure passwords are kept secret and changed at appropriate times	5
	B	ensure computer hardware and program disks are kept securely located	5
	C	identify potential risks to data from different sources and take steps to resolve or minimise them	5
	D	maintain security and confidentiality of data at all times	5
	E	understand and implement relevant legal regulations	5

Assessment Tasks

ASSESSMENT SCENARIO

Note: this Assessment is an adaptation and expansion of Student Activity 14.3 in Osborne Books' 'Costing & Reports Tutorial' (pages 358-359).

the business

Your name is Owen Gerrard and you work as an accounts assistant for Anne Field Enterprises, a sole trader business which operates two sports shops in the North West, one in Liverpool and one in Southport. You work in the Liverpool office.

consolidating figures

You are currently collecting the quarterly financial figures for the two branches so that you can consolidate them into a single profit and loss account.

The figures provided by the two branches are shown below. They include net transfers of stock at cost price between the two shops. Your line manager has told you that these transfers, which are included among the sales and purchases, should not be included in the consolidated figures.

The records from the Liverpool shop show that £200 of stock was sent to the Southport branch on 30 June. This stock in transit was not recorded in the Southport records until 2 July.

Anne Field Enterprises: Profit and Loss Account data for 3 months ended 30 June 2004

	Liverpool Branch		Southport Branch	
	£	£	£	£
Sales		120,000		100,500
Transfers to Southport at cost		5,100		-
		125,100		
Opening stock	56,000		46,000	
Purchases	61,000		53,000	
Transfers from Liverpool at cost	-		4,900	
	117,000		103,900	
Less closing stock	52,500		48,500	
Cost of goods sold		64,500		55,400
Gross Profit		60,600		45,100
Overheads		48,000		39,400
Net Profit		12,600		5,700

You note from the records that the combined profit and loss account figures for the two shops for the same period in 2003 were as follows:

	£
Sales	185,000
Cost of goods sold	112,000
Gross profit	73,000
Overheads	62,000
Net profit	11,000

running the computer system

Another of your tasks is to take responsibility for the running of a new computer system which has recently been installed by a computer consultancy firm in the Liverpool office. This networked system, which links directly with the Southport office, provides:

- a computer accounting facility – combining sales ledger, purchases ledger, main (nominal) ledger, order processing, invoicing, and producing a variety of management reports
- spreadsheet – useful for analysing performance figures
- word processing – with standard files set up in the 'house style' of the business for memos, letters, faxes, short reports
- email management

Anne Field, the owner, is anxious that her investment in this system is well looked after. She asks you that routines for back-up and checking are established and that any new members of staff are well briefed on the operation of the system and the need to maintain the security of data held on computer file.

SUMMARY OF TASKS

Tasks	Activity
1	system checks
2-4	using a spreadsheet and a word processed report to analyse comparative sales figures
5	preparing a word processed guide for the operation of a computer system

TASK 1: SYSTEM CHECKS

Anne has produced the checklist shown on the next three pages for the visual checks and other routines her staff have to carry out. The checks should be made when the staff start up the computer system on arrival in the morning and when they close it down at the end of the day. You are to:

- carry out the same checks when you operate your computer system

- sign and date each check

- provide the information where requested and make any comments if appropriate

If any checks do not apply to your system, you should state 'N/A' in the comments box and give an appropriate reason.

CHECK	Hardware components in place and properly connected?
Date	
Signature	
Comments	

CHECK	Computer system plugged into mains and power on?
Date	
Signature	
Comments	

CHECK	Internet access plugged in (if appropriate)?
Date	
Signature	
Comments	

CHECK	Equipment and cabling complying with Health & Safety Regulations?
Date	
Signature	
Comments	

CHECK	Use password to enter computer system
Date	
Signature	

State whether system is standalone or networked ....

Comments

CHECK	Use password to access software
Date	
Signature	
Comments	

CHECK	Backing-up your work on close down
Date	
Signature	

What data storage medium do you use for your back-up? ....

Comments

CHECK	Close down
Date	
Signature	

What procedures did you carry out to close down the computer system safely?

If you had to leave the computer system running when you had finished your work, what procedures did you carry out with the software and hardware?

TASK 2: CONSOLIDATING THE PROFIT FIGURES

You are to consolidate the figures from the two shops (see page 173) into a profit and loss account for the business for the three months ended 30 June 2004.

You should make the necessary adjustments to exclude transfers of stock, and stock in transit.

No further adjustments need be made.

Note: Tasks 3,4 and 5 involve the operation of various types of software. It is important that you save and back up your work to a suitably named file. Print out your work as indicated and retain the printouts.

TASK 3: ANALYSING THE FIGURES ON A SPREADSHEET

Draw up a spreadsheet setting out comparative figures for the two years (see page 174 for previous year figures). There should be rows for:

- combined sales for the two branches
- cost of goods sold
- gross profit
- gross profit percentage
- overheads
- net profit
- net profit percentage (percentages should be calculated to two decimal places).

You will need to enter formulas as appropriate to make the necessary calculations. Print out the finished spreadsheet.

Then extract from the spreadsheet and print out a compound bar chart showing for the two years:

- sales revenue
- gross profit
- net profit

TASK 4: WORD PROCESSING A REPORT

You are to word process a short report in the house style of the business (ask your Tutor for guidance).

The report should comment on the comparative quarterly performance of the two shops over the two years.

The report should contain features such as bold text, underlines and bullet points. It could also include data imported from the spreadsheet such as the table of figures and a pasted copy of the compound bar chart.

TASK 5: GUIDELINES FOR OPERATION OF A COMPUTER SYSTEM

Anne also asks you to write a short guide to the operation of the new computer system.

The object of this task is to provide the background knowledge needed by employees joining the company.

Anne would like the guide to be word processed and set out in sections, as shown below.

Each section should be headed up as indicated and use should be made where possible of of bold text, underlined text, bullet points and tables.

1 Passwords
- why are passwords used and how are they kept secret?
- how does the business restrict access to certain types of computer data?
- when does the business need to change passwords?

2 Security
- how can computer hardware be kept secure?
- what are the risks to computer software and how can it be protected?
- what are the risks to computer data – eg corruption, theft, illegal copying, breaches of confidentiality – and how can they be avoided?

3 Back-up policy
Describe the data back-up system of the company.

4 Legal background
What laws and regulations affect the operation of a computer system? For example:
- Health & Safety (including VDU regulations)
- software copyright
- protection of personal data
- retention of documents

5 Getting help
What can go wrong with a computer system? For example:
- hardware breakdown
- software failure
- data corruption

What should done and whom should be contacted when something goes wrong?

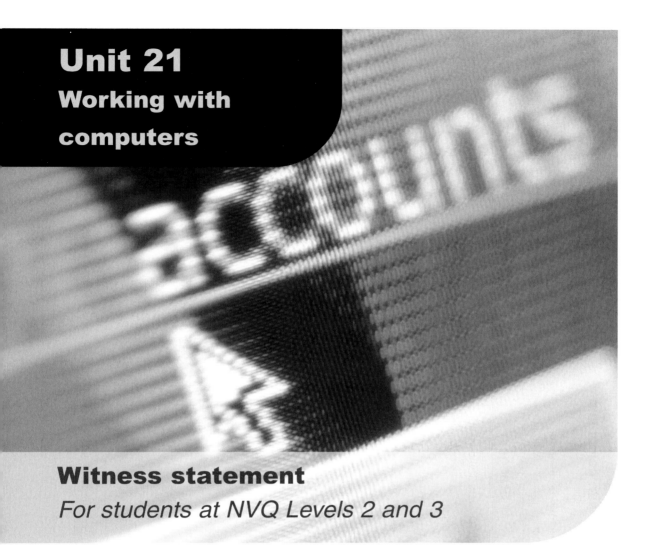

Unit 21
Working with computers

Witness statement
For students at NVQ Levels 2 and 3

- This checklist is suitable for use as a witness statement by a line manager (supervisor) in the workplace. These pages may be photocopied.

- Note that this statement should be supported by an explanation by the student of what he or she did to show competence in each of the performance criteria. This explanation should be supported by any documentary evidence produced, signed by the line manager (supervisor).

- It is important to check that any workplace evidence produced is not confidential in nature.

- This supporting material will also demonstrate the student's coverage of the underlying knowledge and understanding.

- The form itself is based on the performance criteria. It also shows – in the middle column – any range requirements. The right-hand column is for the comments of the line manager, who will also be required to sign the last page of the form.

WITNESS STATEMENT – Unit 21: Working with computers

Student ....

performance criteria	✓	range	✓	comment
21.1 Use computer systems and software		hardware components		
A perform initial **visual safety checks** and power up the **computer system**		plugs		
		cables		
		interfaces		
		for . . .		
		standalone PC		
		networked system		
B use **passwords** to gain access to the **computer system** where limitations on access to data is required		system		
		software		
C access, save and print data files and exit from relevant software				
D use appropriate file names and save work				
E back up work carried out on a computer system to suitable storage media at regular intervals				

WITNESS STATEMENT – Unit 21: Working with computers

page 2

Student ....

performance criteria	✓	range	✓	comment
21.1 Use computer systems and software				
F close down the computer without damaging the **computer system**		standalone networked		
G seek immediate assistance when **difficulties** occur		hardware failure software failure data corruption		
21.2 Maintain the security of data				
A ensure passwords are kept secret and changed at **appropriate times**		on a regular basis disclosure suspected		
B ensure computer hardware and program disks are kept securely located				

WITNESS STATEMENT – Unit 21: Working with computers

Student ....

performance criteria	✓	range	✓	comment

21.2 Maintain the security of data
 	
C identify **potential risks** to data from different **sources** and take steps to resolve or minimise them
		risks: corruption
		           loss
		           illegal copying
		sources: internal
		           external
		           viruses
		           poor storage
		           theft		

D maintain **security** and **confidentiality** of data at all times		back-up copies secure storage passwords		
E understand and implement relevant **legal regulations**		Health & Safety VDU regulations data protection law Document retention		

I confirm that I have observed this student carrying out the tasks indicated above (pages 1 to 3) in a competent manner.

Signed ....   Organisation..   date ....
(Assessor/Line Manager)

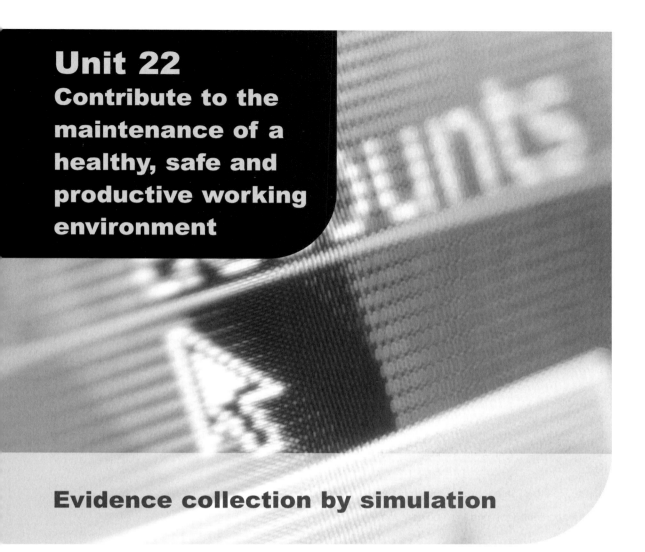

Unit 22
Contribute to the maintenance of a healthy, safe and productive working environment

Evidence collection by simulation

- Unit 22 requires the production of evidence, where possible, from the student's own workplace or from a workplace to which the student has access. This could include a work experience placement, the workplace of a friend or family member, a voluntary organisation or the Centre where the student is being trained.

- There will be situations, however, where the student is unable to obtain this evidence. The material which follows is included for the benefit of students who are not able to collect evidence for a particular performance criterion from the workplace.

- Simulated activities are provided for all of the performance criteria of Unit 22 and are designed around two Case Studies based on an Accounts office scenario.

Element 22.1
Monitor and maintain a safe, healthy and
secure working environment

SCENARIO AND TASKS

Rashid has just started work at Purbeck Vitanetics, a company which develops new drugs for the pharmaceutical industry. Rashid has been appointed an assistant in the Accounts Department.

Performance criterion A

Make sure you read, comply with and have up-to-date information on the health, safety and security requirements and procedures for your workplace.

situation

On Rashid's first day his line manager is giving him induction training. This involves being shown where things are in the building and in his own department. One aspect of the induction training is an introduction to Health & Safety and the security procedures of the company. Rashid is shown, and has explained to him:

- the Health & Safety poster, which he is told to study

- the accident book and the accident forms

- the first aid box

- the Health & Safety Policy, which he is asked to read in his spare time and to sign when he has finished reading it

- the written security procedures, which explain about issues such as locking up and dealing with strangers on the premises

Tasks

1 Describe the purpose of the Health & Safety poster, and explain what it shows.

2 Describe the contents of the Health & Safety Policy.

3 List the details that should be entered in the Accident Book.

Performance criterion B

Make sure that the procedures are being followed and report any that are not to the relevant person.

situation

In his first week at work, Rashid notices that the windows of the department are not locked when he arrives in the morning. He is sure that the security procedures mentioned that all windows should be locked overnight.

Rashid also notices that a colleague has written the system password to his computer workstation on a Post-it note and stuck the note on his computer monitor. Rashid wonders if this is really such a good idea.

Task

State what action you would advise Rashid to take in these two situations.

Performance criterion C

Identify and correct any hazards that you can deal with safely, competently and within the limits of your authority.

Performance criterion D

Promptly and accurately report any hazards that you are not allowed to deal with to the relevant person and warn other people who may be affected.

situation

Rashid notices a number of potential hazards in the office:

(a)   His colleague Jen's filing cabinet bottom drawer is left open in such a way that someone could easily fall over it.

(b)   A power cable to his desk trails over the floor for a couple of metres.

(c)   Rashid notices that some of the office computer monitors, including his, are flickering. They are causing the operators to complain of eyestrain.

(d)   On Thursday morning Rashid notices that the office is uncomfortably cold. People are complaining but nobody is actually doing anything about it. He checks a thermometer on the wall and sees that it is reading 14° Celsius.

Tasks

1   Identify the two potential hazards where Rashid can take action within the limits of his authority.

In each case, state what the potential danger is and what Rashid can do to rectify the situation.

2   Identify the two potential hazards which Rashid should refer to his line manager.

In each case, state what the potential danger is and how the hazard is covered under Health & Safety regulations.

Performance criterion E
Follow your organisation's emergency procedures promptly, calmly and efficiently.

Performance criterion G
Complete any health and safety records legibly and accurately.

situation

One of Rashid's tasks is to help Samantha with the opening of the post. Rashid gets on well with Samantha, but finds her a rather nervous person to work with. She is always telling him about the time they received a suspect package through the post which they thought was a letter bomb from 'animal rights' protestors. They had called the emergency services at the time and had the package destroyed.

One morning, Rashid hands Samantha a package which looks suspicious. She turns pale and falls down in a faint. Unfortunately she is holding the letter opener at the time – it is sharp and she gashes her hand as she falls, causing serious bleeding.

Later in the day, a routine fire drill is held. There is some confusion among the Accounts staff about which fire exit to use and where the meeting point is. One employee stays behind because he is taking an important telephone call.

On another occasion Rashid notices a person he does not recognise looking suspiciously at some files. The staff have recently had a notice published on the company intranet warning them about the possibility of intruders on the premises, trying to find out about the company's research projects. The notice pointed out that an intruder could be identified because he or she would be unlikely to have the plastic ID card that employees carry around with them at work.

Tasks (pc E)

1 Explain what Rashid should do about the package and also about Samantha, who is on the floor and bleeding profusely.

2 Describe (using bullet points) the features of a fire drill in the workplace. Explain what employees would normally be expected to do and mention any signs that would be displayed to assist the procedure.

3 An intruder would be a serious breach of security in the workplace. Describe the steps that would be taken by Rashid to deal with the suspicious person looking at the files.

Task (pc G)

Complete the accident report form in the accident book for Samantha's gashed hand. A suitable form is provided on the next page. Make up any names and other details as appropriate.

Accident Report

Full name of injured person _____

Job Title _____   Department _____

Date of accident _____   Time _____

Location _____

Details of accident

Injury sustained

Witnesses
Name   Job title   Department

Action Taken

Further action necessary

Reported by _____   Reported to _____

Signature _____   Date _____

Performance criterion F

Identify and recommend opportunities for improving health, safety and security to the responsible person

situation

Rashid is tall — well over two metres in height — and has an accident in one of the company's corridors. There is a stairway down at one point and a rather low beam. Rashid has had to take care with it before, but today he is in a hurry and bangs his head on the beam. He is not seriously hurt, but thinks he may get a bruise as a result. He feels strongly that the beam is a hazard to taller people and considers that there should be an official note on the beam saying something like 'Low beam – mind your head!'

Task

Advise Rashid on what short-term and long-term action he should take to prevent this type of workplace accident happening again. Draft a memo from Rashid to his line manager recommending appropriate action.

Element 22.2
Monitor and maintain an effective and
efficient working environment

SCENARIO AND TASKS

You work at Legion Press, a busy small printing firm, based in a town centre location. The business has grown and has plenty of work, but the premises are cramped, which is not ideal for health and safety requirements.

You have just been moved to look after the Sales (Debtors) Ledger. Your desk is in the front office, in full view of visitors who call at the reception desk. You sometimes have to answer visitors' queries and cover for the receptionist when she is at lunch. This is no problem, because your sales ledger work means that you know some of the regular customers. Your desk is also next to the area where the printing presses are operating.

Performance criterion A
Organise the work area you are responsible for, so that you and others can work efficiently

Performance criterion B
Organise the work area you are responsible for, so that it meets your organisation's requirements and presents a positive image of yourself and your team

situation

Your line manager, Debs Heath, gives you initial training for your job and says:

'I am sure you realise that it is important to organise yourself in your work area. Accuracy is so important when you are dealing with customer accounts. We can't have statements being sent to the wrong customer or chasers not being sent out. You will need to use your filing and diary system efficiently so that you know what is going on, and also so that, when you are off on holiday, your stand-in will be able to find all the information easily.

You will also see that your desk is in full public view. I know that this is not ideal, but it is important to remember that you will be seen by customers and also by new clients, so you will have to give a good image of Legion Press to anyone who comes in!'

Task (pc A)

What does Debs mean by a 'work area'? Describe six aspects of a well-organised work area.

Task (pc B)

Write a numbered checklist of what you can do to organise your work area and give a positive impression of yourself and Legion Press.

Performance criterion C
Identify conditions around you that interfere with effective working

Performance criterion D
Put right any conditions that you can deal with safely, competently, within the limits of your authority and with the agreement of other relevant people

Performance criterion E
Promptly and accurately report any other conditions to the relevant person

situation

Your desk, as well as being visible to the visiting public, is next to the area where the printing presses are sited. There is a sliding door between your desk and this area, and unfortunately the door is jammed half-open. As a result, you can hear the noise of the presses, the radio that the operators listen to, and the sound of their voices shouting to each other over the noise of the presses.

Another problem affecting your work area is the light. The main window, which looks over the car park, has blinds, and every morning when you come in, they are closed. The receptionist says she likes subdued lighting and doesn't want people looking in at her all the time from the outside. As a result of the poor light your eyes are getting very tired by the end of the day.

Task (pc C)

Explain what you understand by the phrase 'effective working'.
What are the conditions at Legion Press which prevent you from working effectively?

Task (pc D)

Identify the problem with working conditions which you could put right yourself, after obtaining the agreement of other relevant people. Explain how you would go about obtaining that agreement.

Task (pc E)

Identify the problem with working conditions which you cannot sort out yourself, but will have to refer to your line manager, Debs. Describe what you think the solution to the problem would be.

Performance criterion F

Use and maintain equipment in accordance with manufacturer's instructions and your organisation's procedures

situation

Your work involves you using the office photocopier – eg copying invoices to fax out, copying documents such as purchase orders. During the course of a working week you encounter the following problems:

(a)   the paper jam light comes on

(b)   the photocopier breaks down and the 'maintenance' light comes on

(c)   you find a confidential staff record left on the machine by mistake

Task

Explain what action you would take in each of the three cases outlined above. State in your answer whether or not you would deal with the problem yourself.

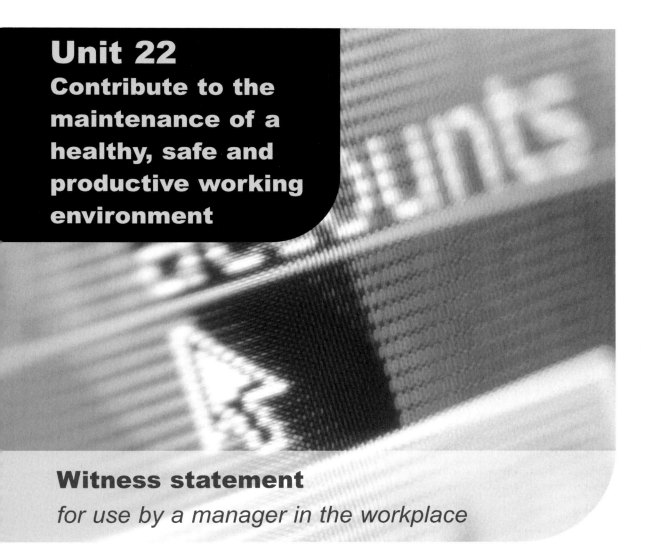

Unit 22
Contribute to the maintenance of a healthy, safe and productive working environment

Witness statement
for use by a manager in the workplace

- This checklist is suitable for use as a witness statement by a line manager (supervisor) in the workplace. These pages may be photocopied.

- Note that this statement should be supported by an explanation by the student of what he or she did to show competence in each of the performance criteria. This explanation should be supported by any documentary evidence produced, signed by the line manager (supervisor).

- It is important to check that any workplace evidence produced is not confidential in nature.

- This supporting material will also demonstrate the student's coverage of the underlying knowledge and understanding.

- The form itself is based on the performance criteria. It also shows – in the middle column – any range requirements. The right-hand column is for the comments of the line manager, who will also be required to sign the last page of the form.

WITNESS STATEMENT – UNIT 22: Contribute to the maintenance of a healthy, safe and productive working environment

Student ....

performance criteria	✓	range	✓	comment
22.1 Monitor and maintain a safe, healthy and secure working environment				
A Make sure you read, comply with and have up-to-date information on the health, safety and security requirements and procedures for your workplace				
B Make sure that the procedures are being followed and report any that are not to the relevant person				
C Identify and correct any hazards that you can deal with safely, competently and within the limits of your authority				
D Promptly and accurately report any hazards that you are not allowed to deal with to the relevant person and warn other people who may be affected				

page 2

WITNESS STATEMENT – UNIT 22: Contribute to the maintenance of a healthy, safe and productive working environment

Student ....

performance criteria	✓	range	✓	comment
22.1 Monitor and maintain a safe, healthy and secure working environment				
E Follow your organisation's emergency procedures promptly, calmly and efficiently		illness		
		accidents		
		fires		
		other reasons to evacuate the premises (eg bomb threat)		
		breaches of security		
F Identify and recommend opportunities for improving health, safety and security to the responsible person				
G Complete any health and safety records legibly and accurately				

WITNESS STATEMENT – UNIT 22: Contribute to the maintenance of a healthy, safe and productive working environment

Student ....

performance criteria	✓	range	✓	comment
22.2 Monitor and maintain an effective and efficient working environment A Organise the work area you are responsible for, so that you and others can work efficiently				
B Organise the work area you are responsible for, so that it meets your organisation's requirements and presents a positive image of yourself and your team				
C Identify conditions around you that interfere with effective working				
D Put right any conditions that you can deal with safely, competently, within the limits of your authority and with the agreement of other relevant people				

WITNESS STATEMENT – UNIT 22: Contribute to the maintenance of a healthy, safe and productive working environment

page 4

Student ....

performance criteria	✓	range	✓	comment
22.2 Monitor and maintain an effective and efficient working environment				
E Promptly and accurately report any other conditions to the relevant person				
F Use and maintain equipment in accordance with manufacturer's instructions and your organisation's procedures				

I confirm that I have observed this student carrying out the tasks indicated above (pages 1 to 4) in a competent manner.

Signed .... Organisation... date ....
(Assessor/Line Manager)

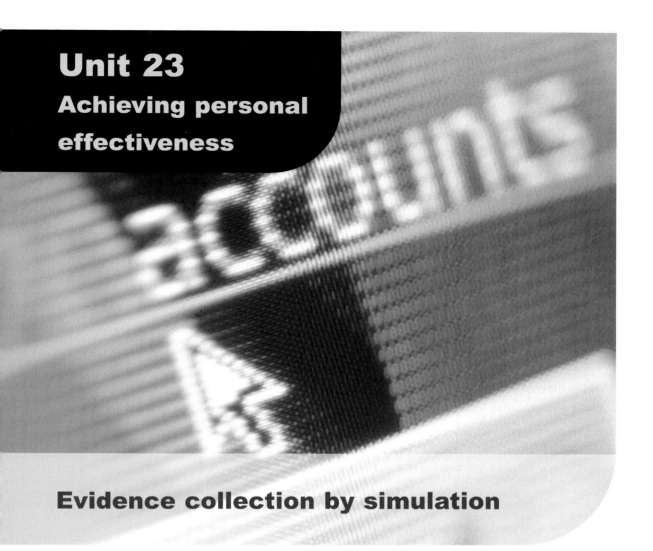

Unit 23
Achieving personal effectiveness

Evidence collection by simulation

introduction

- Unit 23 requires the production of evidence, where possible, from the student's own workplace or from a workplace to which the student has access. This could include a work experience placement, the workplace of a friend or family member, a voluntary organisation or the Centre where the student is being trained.

- There will be situations, however, where the student is unable to obtain this evidence. The material which follows is included for the benefit of students who are not able to collect evidence for a particular performance criterion from the workplace.

- Activities are written – for the first two elements – around a variety of Case Studies based on an office scenario.

- Evidence for Element 23.3, which requires a career development plan, may be generated from work carried out at a teaching centre.

Element 23.1
Plan and organise your own work

SCENARIO AND TASKS

Jim is an accounts and administrative assistant at Crême-de-la-Crême Catering – a company known in the trade as 'CCC'. The company specialises in private events such as wedding receptions and also in hospitality events for other businesses at prime locations, including conference centres, football, rugby and cricket clubs.

Jim is an experienced employee and carries out a wide variety of duties, including sales order processing, payroll and generally assisting the management of CCC.

Performance criterion A
Identify and prioritise tasks according to organisational procedures and regulatory requirements

It is Monday morning. Jim looks at the tasks he has to carry out:

- open and distribute the mail for the department
- prepare the payroll for running on the computer on Wednesday morning
- process the day's sales orders received (cut off time for completion 15.00)
- print out sales figures for the Sales Manager's lunchtime meeting that day
- sort out a leaving collection for Sid Heath, who is leaving next week

Task

Sort Jim's tasks into an order of priority.

Number the tasks and explain in each case why you are giving the task that level of priority.

Performance criterion B
Recognise changes in priorities and adapt resources allocations and work plans accordingly.

situation
At 10.05 on the Monday, the Sales Director rings through to Jim to say that she is meeting a customer later that day. Could she please have account details of the customer and also a provisional quotation for a corporate hospitality event for 50 people at the local rugby club?

Task

Describe how the list of priorities in Task A would change as a result of the Sales Director's request.

Performance criterion C

Use appropriate planning aids to plan and monitor work progress.

situation

On Tuesday Jim meets with his line manager, Ramjit, and other colleagues, to discuss work priorities for the next month. The volume of work has increased and deadlines – both short-term and long-term – have to be met.

The line manager, Ramjit, is concerned that the office is not organised effectively. Deadlines have recently been missed and customers disappointed.

Task

Describe the planning aids that could be used by Jim and his colleagues in the office:

(a)   for day-to-day planning

(b)   for longer term planning, including working out what resources will be needed, and when

---

Performance criterion D

Identify, negotiate and co-ordinate relevant assistance to meet specific demands and deadlines.

Performance criterion E

Report anticipated difficulties in meeting deadlines to the appropriate person.

situation

Jim has been asked to co-ordinate the planning of the hospitality event at the rugby club by the Sales Director.

The event is taking place on the evening of Friday 13 June. It is now 3 June. Jim is getting increasingly worried because he is not going to meet his deadlines.

He has to organise the supplies of food and drink, and staffing, but is having problems with these. He has been working long hours and he has fallen behind with his other tasks.

The final blow came when the Rugby Club telephoned to say that that CCC would not be able to hire the main and prestigious hospitality suite that they had asked for.

Task

What action should Jim take to solve his problems? What help can he ask for? What information will he need to get together to enable people to help him? Write down your recommendations.

Performance criterion F
Check that work methods and activities conform to legal and regulatory requirements and organisational procedures.

situation
During the course of a day, Jim is asked a number of questions by his colleagues:

(a)   Jason asks if he could borrow the office disks for a popular spreadsheet program. He wants to use them at home to help with his accounting studies.

(b)   Kulvinder deals with the sending off of the statutory (ie required by law) Company Annual Return. She tells Jim that it has not yet been completed, but is due at Companies House in Cardiff tomorrow at the latest. She says that she has a lot of work on today, and would it matter if it waited another day – after all it is just a form.

Task

Explain what Jim's response should be to these two requests. Give reasons for your answers, quoting any law or regulations that may be applicable.

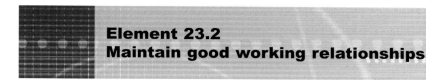

Element 23.2
Maintain good working relationships

SCENARIO AND TASKS

Helen is a senior accounts assistant working for Fellows Consultancy, a company that specialises in offering design consultancy to businesses and other organisations. The company runs a full suite of computer applications on a network system: word processing, spreadsheets, database, email management and web browser.

Helen's main role in the company is overseeing the sales and purchase ledger functions. She is occasionally asked to help carry out specific project work. She often thinks that she should be promoted to line manager because of her success in this type of work.

In the past, Fellows Consultancy has relied on an old computer accounting program which it has had for over ten years and which works, but has its limitations. The management of the company has now decided to introduce a new Sage system, which is flexible and powerful. The transition to the new software will, however, involve a substantial investment in staff time and in training.

Performance criterion A

Communicate with other people clearly and effectively, using your organisation's procedures.

situation

Helen has been appointed to oversee the day-to-day requirements of the transfer. It is a role which will require organisational skills, the ability to run a team of five people and sort out any inter-personal problems that arise. It will also mean liaising with customers and suppliers, as the documentation they will receive will change in format and frequency.

Helen has a wide choice of communication methods that she will be able to use when running this project. Each method used will depend on the type of message she needs to get across and also the type of person involved – either someone who is familiar with the subject matter, or someone who is not. The communication methods include:

- face-to-face communication (eg meetings, interviews)
- telephone
- fax
- email
- word processed documents

Task

Study the list of communication methods on the previous page and write down examples of communication methods Helen is likely to use for:

(a)   people, such as colleagues, who are likely to be familiar with what is required by an integrated computer accounting system

(a)   people, such as customers, who may not be familiar with Sage systems and who will need to be told about the new system

For each example of communication method, give details of the practical situations in which the type of communication is used.

Performance criterion B

Discuss and agree realistic objectives, resources, working methods and schedules and in a way that promotes good working relationships

Performance criterion C

Meet commitments to colleagues within agreed timescales

situation

Helen has decided to hold a series of meetings with the five members of the team. She realises that it is important to:

• set objectives

• find out what resources are available, in terms of people and time

• decide who does what

• establish realistic deadlines

This will all be achieved through teamwork. It will be up to Helen to make sure that everyone can make a contribution to the planning process. It will also be up to Helen to sort out any team-working problems such as rivalries and backbiting.

Tasks (pcs B & C)

1   Describe four important benefits of working in a team.

2   When a team is set up for the first time, what does it need to establish in terms of objectives, resources, working methods and schedules? Give detailed examples of these four factors from a team with which you are familiar (any form of team). Using your example of a team, explain why it is important for team members to keep to timescales and deadlines.

3   List the qualities of an ideal team member.

4   Describe three different 'types' of team member and relate them to your own experience of teams.

Note: the background to these two performance criteria is given in Chapter 8 of this book. It is important to read this chapter before attempting these tasks. It is also important to relate the theory to your own experience of working in teams – for example work teams, sports teams (soccer, basketball) – even the family is a team which sets objectives and has its own particular personal problems!

Performance criterion D

Offer assistance and support where colleagues cannot meet deadlines, within your own work constraints and other commitments.

situation

Helen's team has now established its objectives and set its deadlines. The team plans to complete the transition to the Sage system within four weeks. The activities involved include:

- setting up the sales, purchase and nominal (main) ledgers on the new system
- setting up new administrative systems, eg for dealing with banking transactions, document checking and so on
- advising customers and suppliers about the changes
- advising other Fellows Consultancy employees about the changes
- running staff training

All runs well for two weeks, when one of the team, Tania, who is responsible for the re-inputting of the data into the Sage system, is off sick for four days. As a result the program begins to run behind schedule. When Tania returns she tells Helen that she is pregnant, but there is a problem with the pregnancy and she will have to take sick leave for the next month. Helen reckons that there is three days' work to be done before the project gets back on schedule. Helen herself is fast at inputting, but she has a fairly full diary.

Task

What support can Helen herself offer to the team in both a practical and a personal way to help with the pressures of added work and delayed deadlines? Describe what you would do in her position.

Performance criterion E

Find workable solutions for any conflicts and dissatisfaction which reduce personal and team effectiveness

Performance criterion F

Follow organisational procedures if there are difficulties in working relationships that are beyond your authority or ability to resolve, and promptly refer them to the appropriate person

Performance criterion G

Treat others courteously and work in a way that shows respect for other people

situation

Helen has now encountered a personal conflict within the team which she is unable to resolve by herself. The extra workload caused by the departure of Tania has meant that two of the team members are under a great deal of pressure. The two team members are:

- **Asaf**, a sales ledger assistant. He is a confident and fast worker and the older and more senior of the two. He is always giving his colleagues the benefit of his opinions of how to get things done. His work, however, is not always accurate, as he tends to rush at things to try to get them finished.

- **Kerry**, a slower but more accurate worker. She is Asaf's junior and much quieter than him. She tends to keep her opinions to herself. She can be relied on, but can sometimes take a long time to achieve her objectives.

Problems come to crisis point at a team meeting. They are discussing the allocation of extra inputting work which is needed to be done as a matter of some urgency.

'I really can't take this on!' says an exasperated Asaf, 'I'm already working overtime as it is! Why can't Kerry do it? She must have more time than me. This whole project is becoming a real pain in the neck!'

Kerry looks down and bursts into tears.

Asaf walks out of the meeting saying to Helen, 'You are just going to have to sort this out. I have had enough!'

Task (pc F)
Describe how the difficulties in working relationships are caused in this case by:

    (a) differences in personality

    (b) differences in working style

    (c) status of employees

    (d) the demands of work

Task (pcs E & G)
Describe how Helen might be able to solve the dispute without referring the problem to her Manager, Alun Davies. How should she treat the team members in order to win them over to her proposed solution?

Task (pc F)
If Helen is unable to resolve the problem on her own, what should her next steps be?

Performance criterion H
Ensure data protection requirements are followed strictly and also maintain confidentiality of information relating to colleagues.

situation

A customer telephones Helen and asks her for the banking details of one of Fellows Consultancy's employees, as he says he wants to pay a cheque into the employee's account.

Task
State what Helen's reply should be and explain why she has to reply in this way.

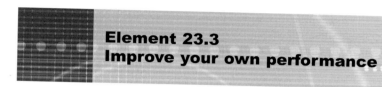

Element 23.3
Improve your own performance

SCENARIO AND TASKS

Element 23.3 is treated differently from the other elements in this Unit. It requires you to identify your own career development needs and then to write and review a career development plan.

If you are in employment, this will be relatively straightforward. If you are not in work, the process will involve examining the type of work you would like to do and setting targets for obtaining it.

The element therefore falls into two distinct parts:

1 deciding where you are in your career and where you want your career to go (pcs A, B, C, D)

2 reviewing your performance and your career needs (pcs E, F, G, H)

Both stages require you to discuss your present or intended career with others. If you are in work, this can take place as part of the standard appraisal process; if you are not in work the discussion can take place with a tutor or careers advisor.

We have structured previous evidence guidance with 'situations' and 'tasks' related to specific performance criteria. In this element the situation is *your* situation, and so the structure is purely task-based.

PART 1: WRITING THE PLAN

Performance criteria covered:

A **identify your own development needs by taking into consideration your current work activities and also your own career goals**

B **define your own development objectives and, where necessary, agree them with the appropriate person**

C **research appropriate ways of acquiring new skills and knowledge**

D **ensure that development opportunities are realistic and achievable in terms of resources and support from relevant persons**

Tasks

The overall task is to prepare a career development plan.

This involves a number of stages which can be basically summed up as:

'Where am I now? Where do I want to go? How am I going to get there?'

Suggested tasks are listed below.

Note that you should discuss the whole process with other people. Depending on your circumstances these might include managers undertaking appraisals at work, training advisors and tutors at a training centre.

You might also gather information and get advice from training courses you have been on and by studying training and career advice literature.

1   Describe exactly where you stand now in terms of your career: are you in work, or are you planning to get a job and start a career?

2   If you are in work or planning to get a job, decide whether you are fully trained for the job and whether you have the necessary qualifications.

3   Define your objectives – what do you want to achieve – in the short-term (eg 6-9 months) and the longer term (eg up to five years)?

Objectives might include: specific on-the-job training, external qualifications and areas of knowledge relating to the job.

4   You will need to carry out research into ways of obtaining these new skills and knowledge and will need to provide evidence of this research. The career development process involves:

- deciding on a qualification eg AAT, ACCA, CIMA, CIPFA
- finding suitable courses (eg at a college or with a private training provider),
- researching the internet sites of qualification providers (eg www.aat.org.uk) and other bodies related to the planned career
- reading associated journals, eg Accounting Technician (www.accountingtechnician.co.uk)
- reading relevant books and study material (see www.osbornebooks.co.uk)
- using IT-based training aids
- talking to colleagues who are also training and taking qualifications
- talking to and observing colleagues who are expert in the area of work you are targetting – this could be at the workplace or at a college where you meet people in the same area of work as yourself

5   Draw up an action plan which contains defined objectives and a planned timescale (initially for 12 months, but also including longer-term targets, eg over five years).

6   Discuss your draft plan with other people (eg a workplace manager, a tutor) to ensure that your objectives are realistic and achievable, given the resources you have at your disposal.

PART 2: REVIEWING THE PLAN

Performance criteria covered:

E   review and evaluate your performance and progress and also to agreed timescales

F   monitor your own understanding of developments relating to your job role

G   maintain and develop your own specialist knowledge relevant to your own working environment

H   undertake learning that will help you improve your performance

Tasks

The objective of these four performance criteria is that you should monitor and review your career plan periodically. This will take account of changes in your circumstances and the changing skills and knowledge requirements of your job.

The review process will involve both you and your workplace appraiser/tutor/advisor. The main questions that will be asked are:

'Have I achieved my objectives on time?'

'Have I made the progress I had planned?'

'Are there any other factors and needs that I should now investigate?'

Suggested questions to answer are listed below.

1   How well have I achieved my objectives in the short-term (eg 6-9 months)?

2   Have there been any major changes in my career path which will require changes in the plan?

3   How has my job role developed and changed in the short term?

4   Are there any new training requirements for my present job, eg technological changes, IT developments?

5   What sources of information have I used to keep me up-to-date and inform me about my working environment? For example – my course, the internet, journals, books, information from colleagues and the workplace.

6   What (if any) new objectives should I have to help me improve my competence in the workplace?

---

important note

If you are not in employment, this assessment can be based wholly around the course you are taking, the assumption being that you will eventually get a job. The action plan you write will involve planning your studies and obtaining the qualification. The evidence you produce might include course specifications, schemes of work, diaries, revision timetables, web printouts, photocopies of journal articles and book extracts, records of discussions with tutors and with fellow students.

Unit 23
Achieving personal effectiveness

Witness statement
for use by a manager or assessor

- This checklist is suitable for use as a witness statement by a line manager (supervisor) in the workplace or an assessor. It may be photocopied.

- Note that this statement should be supported by an explanation by the student of what he or she did to show competence in each of the performance criteria. This explanation should be supported by any documentary evidence produced, signed by the line manager (supervisor).

- It is important to check that any workplace evidence produced is not confidential in nature.

- This supporting material will also demonstrate the student's coverage of the underlying knowledge and understanding.

- The form itself is based on the performance criteria. It also shows – in the middle column – any range requirements. The right-hand column is for the comments of the line manager, who will also be required to sign the last page of the form.

WITNESS STATEMENT – Unit 23: Achieving personal effectiveness

Student ....

performance criteria	✓	range	✓	comment
23.1 Plan and organise your own work				
A identify and prioritise **tasks** according to organisational procedures and regulatory requirements		routine tasks unexpected tasks		
B recognise changes in priorities and adapt resources allocations and work plans accordingly				
C use appropriate **planning aids** to plan and monitor work progress		diaries schedules action plans		
D identify, negotiate and co-ordinate relevant assistance to meet specific demands and deadlines				

WITNESS STATEMENT – Unit 23: Achieving personal effectiveness

Student ....

performance criteria	✓	range	✓	comment
23.1 Plan and organise your own work				
E report anticipated difficulties in meeting deadlines to the **appropriate person**		line manager		
		project manager		
		colleague(s) relying on the completion of your work		
F check that work methods and activities conform to legal and regulatory requirements and organisational procedures				

WITNESS STATEMENT – Unit 23: Achieving personal effectiveness

Student ....

performance criteria	✓	range	✓	comment
23.2 Maintain good working relationships A **communicate** with **other people** clearly and effectively, using your organisation's procedures		face-to-face by telephone by fax by email by creating word-processed documents		
		with . . . other people familiar with the subject matter other people not familiar with the subject matter		
B discuss and agree realistic objectives, resources, working methods and schedules and in a way that promotes good working relationships				

WITNESS STATEMENT – Unit 23: Achieving personal effectiveness

Student ....

performance criteria	✓	range	✓	comment
23.2 Maintain good working relationships				
C meet commitments to colleagues within agreed timescales				
D offer **assistance and support** where colleagues cannot meet deadlines, within your own work constraints and other commitments		personal practical		
E find workable solutions for any conflicts and dissatisfaction which reduce personal and team effectiveness				
F follow organisational procedures if there are **difficulties in working relationships** that are beyond your authority or ability to resolve, and promptly refer them to the appropriate person		personality working style status work demands		
G treat others courteously and work in a way that shows respect for other people				
H ensure data protection requirements are followed strictly and also maintain confidentiality of information relating to colleagues				

WITNESS STATEMENT – Unit 23: Achieving personal effectiveness

Student ....

performance criteria	✓	range	✓	comment
23.3 Improve your own performance				
A **identify your own development needs** by taking into consideration your current work activities and also your own career goals		through training through discussions self-study of relevant materials		
B define your own development objectives and, where necessary, agree them with the appropriate person				
C research appropriate **ways of acquiring new skills and knowledge**		courses internet journals/trade publications books through colleagues observation		
D ensure that development opportunities are realistic and achievable in terms of resources and support from relevant persons				

WITNESS STATEMENT – Unit 23: Achieving personal effectiveness

Student ....

performance criteria	✓	range	✓	comment
23.3 Improve your own performance				
E **review and evaluate your performance and progress** and also to agreed timescales		by self in conjunction with others		
F monitor your own understanding of developments relating to your job role				
G maintain and develop your own specialist **knowledge** relevant to your own working environment		courses internet journals/trade publications books through colleagues observation		
H undertake learning that will help you improve your performance				

Unit 23: Achieving personal effectiveness

I confirm that I have observed this student carrying out the tasks indicated above (pages 1-6) in a competent manner.

Student name ....

Signed .... (Assessor/Line Manager)

Organisation...

date ....

Index